THE ROAD

THE ROAD

UPRISING IN WEST PAPUA

JOHN MARTINKUS

Published by Black Inc.,
an imprint of Schwartz Books Pty Ltd
Level 1, 221 Drummond Street
Carlton VIC 3053, Australia
enquiries@blackincbooks.com
www.blackincbooks.com

9781760642426 (paperback)
9781743821350 (ebook)

A catalogue record for this book is available from the National Library of Australia

Cover design by Akiko Chan
Text design and typesetting by Akiko Chan
Map (p. xiii) by John Waddingham
All images supplied
Cover image © NurPhoto / Getty Images

To all the West Papuans, dead and alive,
who have dedicated their lives to justice since
the illegal Indonesian takeover of 1961.

To the activists, journalists, health workers,
priests and nuns who have given so much to help
the people of this tormented land, and still do.

CONTENTS

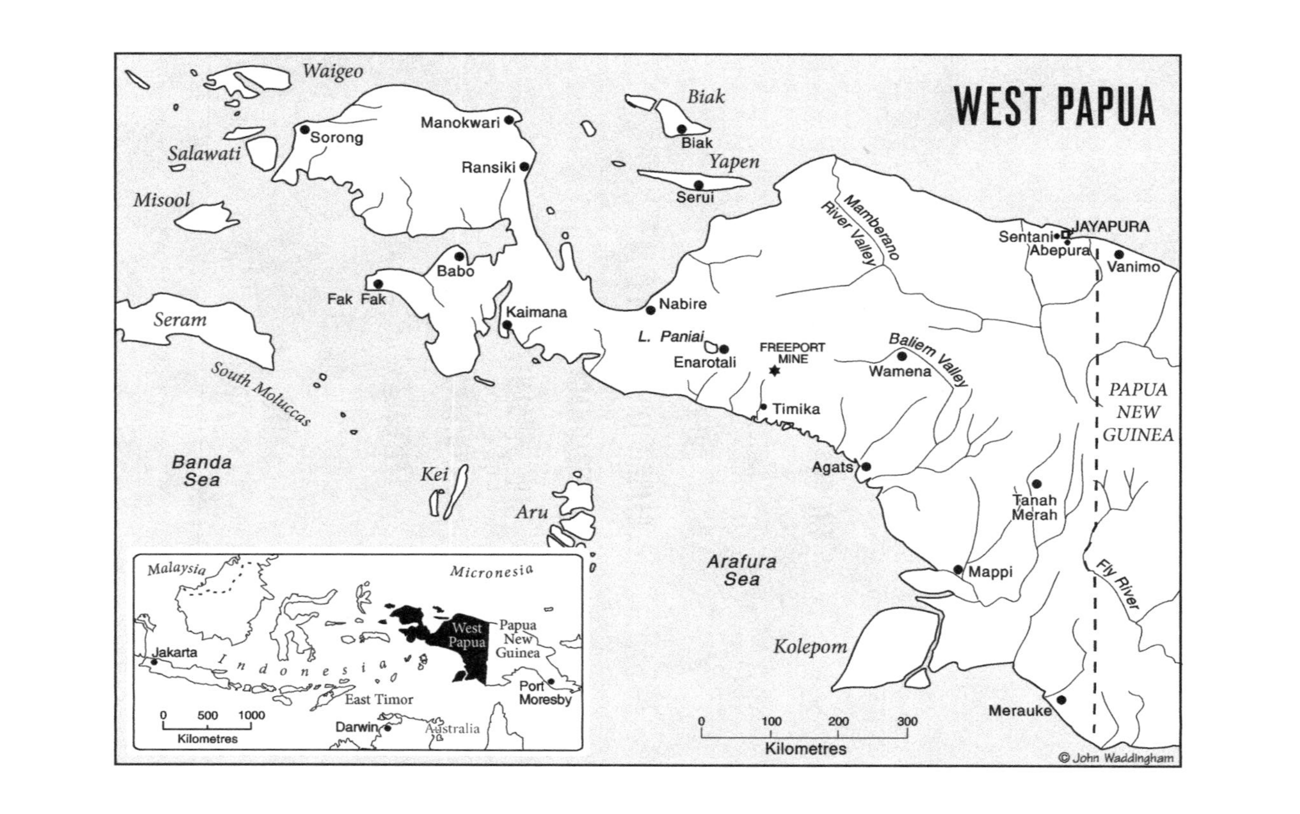
WEST PAPUA
Waigeo
Biak
Biak
Sorong
Manokwari
Ransiki
Salawati
Misool
Yapen
Serui
Mamberano
River Valley
JAYAPURA
Sentani
Abepura
Vanimo
Babo
Fak Fak
Seram
Kaimana
Nabire
L. Paniai
Enarotali
FREEPORT
MINE
Baliem Valley
Wamena
Timika
South Moluccas
PAPUA
NEW
GUINEA
Banda
Sea
Kei
Aru
Agats
Tanah
Merah
Arafura
Sea
Mappi
Fly River
Kolepom
Merauke
0
100
200
300
Kilometres
© John Waddingham
Malaysia
Micronesia
West
Papua
Papua
New
Guinea
Jakarta
Indonesia
Port
Moresby
East Timor
0
500
1000
Kilometres
Darwin
Australia

INTRODUCTION

It was a kind of obsession for the men who had had their first taste of conquering and combat in what was then Dutch New Guinea. They jumped in from aircraft or arrived by landing craft at remote locations to, as they saw it, remove the last vestiges of Dutch colonialism from their domain. They were tough men in unmapped jungle with little idea what they would face: hostile natives, difficult terrain, a lack of supplies. And so, when those 1200 or so Indonesian paratroopers leapt into West Papua in 1961 and '62, they were easily defeated. The Dutch marines rounded them up, with the help of the spear tips and arrows of the local population. One Dutch marine spoke of feeling sick as he watched two ragged Indonesian soldiers be dragged out of the jungle, shot dead on a bridge and their bodies dumped in the river. He saw prisoners delivered to the Papuan auxiliaries. The Papuans saw no point in keeping the prisoners, and besides, it kept the other ones quiet. Starving, sick and with the arses literally rotting out of their fatigues, the Indonesians were paraded in front of the newsreel cameras of the day.

It was a diplomatic fluke and not a military victory that won Indonesia the territory of Dutch New Guinea. But those junior officers who survived their own failed attack later became generals, obsessed with an idea that would justify their suffering and eulogise the dead superiors and comrades of their youth: building the road. The Trans-Papua Highway, which would finally fulfil the Sukarno-era boast of a unified Indonesian nation. 'From Sabang to Merauke', the president would chant to cheering rallies, referring to the easternmost island off the tip of Aceh and the southernmost town in West Papua, the latter barely a day's ride in a tinnie with an outboard to Australia across the Torres Strait. The Trans-Papua Highway would traverse some of the most remote and inhospitable terrain in Asia. An area with mountains so high that it has one of the few equatorial glaciers in the world. A place where people are dying to this day, fighting and fleeing Indonesian military operations.

The plan evolved in the minds of the generals and their civil servants. They would push out from Sorong on the 'bird's head', an important port on the tip of West Papua. They would work down from the next regional town, Manokwari, and out from the capital, Jayapura, both on the north coast. Then, in a pincer movement, they would link and push through to the highlands, through Nduga province to the capital of the isolated Baliem Valley, Wamena. Wamena had only had its first European visitor in 1904; it wasn't until 1920 and 1938 that other expeditions came through.

The Dani and Nduga people who inhabit this part of the West Papuan highlands are different. They are physically tougher, due to their environment of high-altitude jungle and mountains, and they are culturally different as well: centuries of limited contact with the coastal tribes, and internecine fighting and almost ceremonial wars with each other, have bred a very robust people. They refuse to admit their region is part of Indonesia and will not speak Bahasa. They are not people likely to back down. But the generals, with their dream of the road, did not care for the wishes of the Nduga and the Dani. In the words of Indonesian defence minister Ryamizard Ryacudu (a former general with a history of human rights abuses), they would 'crush them'. And now we are witnessing – from a distance, due to restrictions put in place by the generals – what crushing means.

THE END OF THE ROAD

This is a story that covers many years and many trips I made to far-flung parts of Indonesia, mostly in search of conflicts to report on. I wanted to go where no Western journalists were allowed. I started in the mid-1990s in East Timor, now the independent country of Timor Leste, travelling as a tourist because journalists were banned. I hung out there, despite regular casual death threats and constant surveillance. Eventually I got up into the mountains with the pro-independence guerrillas. I hiked quietly with them in the jungle and slept in a tarpaulin-covered hole with branches over the top, hiding from the Indonesian troops who came so close we could hear their boots breaking twigs in the scrub. That band of men were mostly killed or captured the following year, after they attacked and killed thirty Indonesian police in an ambush near their hideout. Their commander, David Alex, was taken alive but never seen again.

I returned to East Timor again and again and, following the fall of the dictator Suharto in May 1998, I was able to stay there permanently and obtain a journalist visa. I covered the rise of the student opposition, reporting on the marches and protests and the inevitable backlash by the Indonesian military and the militias they used as a screen to hide their killing. Weeks that turned into months were spent covering massacres and killings across the provinces. Counting bodies, getting numbers of the dead. Basic reporting, really, but always in the face of threats from the Indonesian military, the police, their intelligence operatives and their militias, as they maintained the fiction that they were simply trying to keep the peace between two warring Timorese sides: the pro-independence movement and the Timorese militia, whom they were arming, organising, paying and driving around, and sometimes impersonating, to massacre their fellow citizens. For the record, Australia went along with this fiction until the final days, when the Timorese voted overwhelmingly for independence and the Indonesian state turned on both the East Timorese – killing those they deemed pro-independence, burning and depopulating their towns and villages – and the foreign community, forcing them to evacuate so they could finish their job without foreign witnesses. It is a modus operandi the Indonesian military used again in Aceh in 2003 and, at the time of writing, is using in West Papua.

During Indonesia's reluctant and destructive and brutal withdrawal from East Timor following the arrival of the Australian-led peace-keeping force, we journalists continued to report on the violence. We travelled to neighbouring West Timor to document the almost one-third of the East Timorese population who had been forcibly evacuated there, driving past the piles of looted televisions, motorbikes, furniture, even electrical wire torn from power poles that rotted in the monsoonal rain just over the border. Then there were the camps – thousands of desperate people being held by the 'militias' as a kind of bargaining chip. Over the next six months, most of them were eventually repatriated to East Timor, but not before many had been raped or killed. In the capital, Kupang, I went to the old expat bar on the waterfront. Teddy's had always been a seedy place full of Australian men drinking in the morning and eyeing off the bored-looking girls. This time there was no one there but myself and a drunk East Timorese soldier from one of the notorious 744 and 745 Battalions, made up of East Timorese with Indonesian officers. They had just killed nuns, a priest, two journalists and many, many civilians as they made their way out of East Timor. He asked me to buy him a drink and rolled a grenade across the bar. I bought the drink, downed mine fast and left.

Ironically, out of this chaos and uncertainty there followed a period of roughly four years when journalists were able to take advantage of a relative freedom in Indonesia. We could visit Aceh, at the far north-western tip of Indonesia, and Papua, in the far south-east, where separatist wars had simmered ever since the territories had been integrated into the Indonesian nation. Both areas had long been banned or heavily restricted to foreign journalists. Entering these regions was difficult and intimidating, with constant document checks, threats of violence and the ever-present surveillance by the Indonesian intelligence services, but it was, for the first time, possible. That is how, as most of my colleagues went to Afghanistan when war broke out in 2001, I ended up in Aceh. And how, when war was mounting in Iraq in 2003, most of my colleagues went there and I ended up in Merauke, Papua. The south-easternmost town in Indonesia. Literally the end of the road.

*

There was not a lot to do in Merauke in 2003. It was under curfew and the streets were empty except for the rare military vehicle, usually just visiting one of the brothels in the town with one of the highest rates of HIV in Indonesia. Two years earlier, on 1 December 2001, the locals had tried to raise the flag of independent West Papua, the Morning Star, with its horizontal blue and white stripes to signify the Dutch colonial influence and the single prominent star to symbolise the morning star that rises over the territory. The police shot and killed seven people, and since then there had been no more trouble in Merauke. The Indonesian military took down the pro-independence security posts, where local men would try to check those coming into their area from the outside, as soon as they were put up.

I couldn't speak to the local independence movement, known as the OPM (Organisasi Papua Merdeka, or the Free Papua Movement). They had fled across the border to Papua New Guinea after their leader, Willem Onde, had been 'disappeared' in 2001. He had started to deal with the Indonesian special forces unit Kopassus in 1997, agreeing to a weapons handover. His reward was a new gun for himself and some money, which he promptly spent. He started hanging around and drinking with the Indonesian officers and never fought them again. But the truce came at a price: when thirteen logging workers, including three South Koreans, were 'kidnapped', supposedly by the OPM fighters under Onde, a large ransom was paid to the Indonesian military and the hostages were released. Future payments were also organised by the logging company for the 'protection' of their workers by the Indonesian military. This was how business was done in West Papua and why the Indonesian military liked it so much there. It was a protection racket that went all the way up to Indonesia's largest taxpayer, the US-run Freeport-McMoRan Grasberg mine, the largest gold mine and second-largest copper mine in the world.

Onde was last seen alive in September 2001, on a motorbike with his assistant on the back. His body and that of his assistant were found by the side of the road four days later. He had been scalped. A passing logging truck had seen Kopassus troops in the area by the road on the day of his death. He had become a pawn in a much larger game. His story is worth telling because it says a lot about how the Indonesian military and the government dealt with West Papua – and still do.

I did get hold of a document that I thought was a major story. It was from the Indonesian Department of Internal Affairs, dated 9 June 2000, and listed independence figure Theys Eluay and Willem Onde as leaders who had to be made to support autonomy. Offering autonomy was the Indonesian plan to dampen West Papuans' calls for independence, placating them with promises of better funding for infrastructure and more involvement of the local leaders in government. It was a plan to head off the calls for independence that had gained momentum following the independence of East Timor. The document was basically a hit list: in the following months and years it would be used as a guide for Indonesian troops in the field – who to watch, who could be bought off and who would just have to be killed.

Theys Eluay, the most charismatic and unifying Papuan leader to emerge from the West Papuan independence movement in years, was killed in 2001, in his car outside Jayapura. On 10 November, he attended a dinner to celebrate Heroes Day, when those Indonesians who had taken part in the takeover of Papua were remembered and celebrated by their countrymen. Over the microphone the police commander wished him a safe trip home when he left around 10 pm. He gave a ride to some Kopassus members who wanted a lift. They killed him by suffocation on the road along the way. His driver was never seen again.

Eventually four Kopassus members were charged with his murder. At their trials, the crime was portrayed as the actions of overzealous troops on the ground. But the document I'd got hold of had come from a meeting of civilian and military leaders in Jakarta. The fact that the program was initiated in a meeting of the civilian interior ministry and military officers revealed that it was endorsed by government. The Kopassus officers, who admitted to the murder, were given sentences of three to three and a half years after several years of trials. At the time of their conviction, the commander of the Indonesian army, General Endriartono Sutarto, said publicly these soldiers should be considered 'heroes', as they had killed in order to maintain the national unity of the Republic. Before his murder, Theys Eluay had been trying to raise the issue of Willem Onde's death down in Merauke. There has never been an investigation into the death of Willem Onde.

When I had the document properly translated, I thought I had a huge scoop. It was verification that if you were a Papuan leader who refused to publicly support autonomy and you were on the list Kopassus had drawn up, you would be killed. I thought it was journalistic gold, but the world's attention was on Iraq and the invasion by the US-led forces. Confirmation that a few murders in remote West Papua were linked to Indonesian government policy simply didn't rate as a news story in Australia, New Zealand, the United Kingdom or Hong Kong, where the outlets I was filing to were located. Their foreign coverage was focused on the big dash across the desert unfolding in the Middle East as the coalition troops prepared to close in on Baghdad. No one ran the story.

*

I didn't have much time left in Merauke and didn't know what to do. There had been some trouble recently on the nearby island of Yos Sudarso, named after the Indonesian commander killed in 1962 when his ship was sunk by the Dutch as he tried to land troops. Locals there have little contact with the outside world and live a very traditional life. Some Indonesian fisherman had approached the island and the locals attacked them with spears. The militarised Indonesian police Brimob (Korps Brigade Mobil) then headed down and shot some people and burned their huts. I was shown photos of dead people wearing grass skirts. There was no attempt at procedure. It being such a remote place, the Indonesians just killed some locals to make a point, as they always did when there was trouble on the island. I thought about going there, but it would have involved hiring a boat and carrying a week's supplies, like some sort of explorer. I didn't have the money.

With one day to go in this town at the end of Indonesia, only 400 kilometres from Australian territory, I decided to take a drive to the Papua New Guinea border just to see it: the end of the road. I hired a small van at the market. The driver was a Javanese who said he had never been the 60 kilometres or so and insisted on taking a friend along. They seemed nervous. The road ran on a levee straight through the surrounding swamps and then red dirt, scrub and some gum trees that made it look like northern Australia.

There were a few military bases set off from the main road and a small village at a crossroads. Close to the border were a few short rows of Javanese-looking houses that seemed out of place in the open ground, like seeing terrace houses in the middle of a swamp. At the border itself there was nothing except a broken picnic chair and a concrete cairn put there by the joint Australian–Indonesian army survey team in 1983. The sealed road stopped abruptly and was met with a small muddy track that led off into the trees. I walked along it for about

2 kilometres with the nervous Javanese following behind me. I was expecting some kind of PNG post or village, but all I found was an old man and two women sitting under a tree. I asked them how far to the next village and they looked at me very seriously and said it was three days and three nights walking, probably more for me. That was it. The end of Indonesia: a muddy track through the wilderness on a random line dictated in Europe in the nineteenth century.

As we drove back to Merauke we passed the monument that proudly stated 'From Sabang to Merauke', with the eagle-like Garuda emblem of the Republic of Indonesia underneath. It seemed the only point to build the road to the border had been to delineate the Indonesian territory, and to supply a few small military posts whose main purpose appeared to be keeping people inside West Papua, rather than keeping others out. The end of the road was just like the end of the road I had visited in Sabang, at the other end of Indonesia – little more than a crumbling ruin in the wilderness in another area long racked by conflict. But still the Indonesians talked of how the road would one day connect up the entire country and everything would be better.

An Indonesian soldier with a small Papuan boy stepped onto the road and flagged us down. They got into the back seat and told the two now-silent Javanese men in the front to keep driving. Intentionally or not, the soldier had the barrel of his M16 pointed at my head as he started speaking in English. 'I am from Kostrad. You know Kostrad. They send us to where it is danger,' he said.

I went to light a cigarette and he grabbed the pack from me. He seemed to know what I was doing – and what I was doing there in particular. The soldier laughed and said he thought I was CIA. 'You know, like James Bond. Ha.' He then started telling me how he had been in East Timor, in Lospalos in 1994 and Suai in 1995. 'Maybe I see you there,' he said, grinning. Then he went on to tell me how he had been in Ambon in 2000 and then in Kalimantan, both places of military-driven ethnic violence at the time. 'They send us to all the hot spots,' he said. 'I would do anything to defend Indonesia. I love Indonesia.'

He was laughing but there was an element of threat in it, and as we drove, the only car on the road through this swampy area at the end of the country, I had a real feeling of dread. It felt as though I had been set up, that the military was going to take this opportunity to issue yet another warning to the foreign press to stay out of their affairs.

I was getting angry with myself for being out there for no real reason. The soldier kept talking about how the Papuan people loved them. The small boy with him laughed at the obvious discomfort of the strange foreigner. The two Javanese in the front were laughing nervously too, as the soldier kept talking about how he would do anything for Indonesia, how he would kill for Indonesia. His gun was still pointed at my head, his finger inside the trigger guard. The safety, I noticed, was off.

He kept referring to places and conflicts I had reported on where he had been present. Times, places, dates. He was laughing and waving around his free arm. It was probably just coincidence due to our similar ages and professions: his job was conducting conflicts in Indonesia, mine was reporting on them. But I genuinely thought that out there in the middle of nowhere, on the darkening road with no one else about, he was going to kill me.

Then, just as suddenly as the soldier had arrived, he banged on the roof of the van and yelled for the driver to stop. There was a flag in the scrub that must have marked his post. He got out, still talking about what he would do to maintain the integrity of his country. The two Javanese in the front relaxed and we sped away. They had been thinking the same thing I had, that the soldier was going to kill me. It happened out there to Papuans all the time.

I left Merauke the next day, flying to Timika then on to Jakarta, and the Indonesian authorities haven't allowed me to return to West Papua since. But back then, as I watched an unmarked 737 taxiing down the runway in Timika with supplies and personnel destined for the Grasberg mine, I thought, This is not going to end well. Over the next few years I would see those same unmarked aircraft in airports in Kabul, Kandahar, Baghdad, Amman and Dubai. The same charter planes that companies, militaries and governments use to deliver cargo and people to places no one else will fly. Colonialism, imperialism, corporate-driven economic exploitation – call it whatever you like but the result is the same: a restful, rebellious, disenfranchised population. It just depends whether you can employ enough security or sufficiently co-opt the local military to get away with it until the resources are extracted. When, a year earlier, I had sat with OPM commander Goliath Tabuni and he'd raised his voice and said they would fight to the death to stop the mine, I knew the conflict would continue. I knew they would, as he declared, 'fight to the death' to stop it. And they have. Now their sons have taken up the fight.

TAKEOVER

On 1 December 1961, the Papuans, alongside the Dutch, raised their Morning Star flag for the first time. In emotional ceremonies, Papuans wept at the sight of their flag being officially raised. They would have a country they could run themselves. They would control their own destiny and resources. They would be independent. It was happening and the Dutch were facilitating it.

The Dutch had argued that West Papua was ethnically distinct from their former colonies in what they called the Dutch East Indies, and therefore should not be part of the new Indonesian nation. They had begun preparing a new generation of social administrators and civil servants to run what they considered would eventually be an independent state. They had a police force, an auxiliary military and a civil service. Australia, undertaking a decolonisation process across the border in Papua New Guinea, was doing the same thing, preparing that nation for independence. Australian prime minister Robert Menzies was a big supporter of the Dutch decolonisation process and transition to independence of what was then known as Dutch New Guinea. Declassified Australian documents reveal that the conservative Menzies government favoured the integration of Dutch New Guinea with Australian-administered Papua New Guinea to be prepared for eventual independence as a united island nation.

The United States had a different idea. As Australian academic Julian McKinlay King wrote in 2019 in his research covering the period:

> With increasing military incursions by Indonesia and no support from their traditional Allies, the Netherlands attempted to have the UN take over the Territory in 1961 via a UN Trusteeship, as available under Article XII of the Charter, in order to 'relinquish sovereignty to the people of Netherlands New Guinea' (General Assembly Plenary Meeting 1016, para 90). The proposal, however, failed to gain the required two-thirds majority in the General Assembly due to Cold War and religious affiliations taking precedence over the legal rights of the West Papuan people. Pressure from the US government over Indonesia's threat to align with Communist Soviet Union was used to coerce the Netherlands into relinquishing the Territory to Indonesia.[1]

President John F. Kennedy supported Sukarno and his new nation of Indonesia in its expansionist campaign in Papua. He pressured the Dutch and the Australians to allow the Indonesians to prevail. The Cold War realities and the US fear of allowing Indonesia to fall into the Soviet sphere meant the Papuan people and their rights were irrelevant. Indonesia's charismatic but sometimes erratic first president, Sukarno, had played his hand well. By agreeing to Soviet aid and military support, he had manoeuvred the United States and, as a result, both Australia and the Netherlands, into supporting his takeover of Papua with the implicit threat he would simply seek help from the Soviets if they didn't.

Throughout the 1960s, the Dutch were nominally still in control but the Indonesians gradually took over administration of the western half of New Guinea. For Sukarno, unity was a point of honour. A fixation. 'Indonesia: From Sabang to Merauke'. Meanwhile, on the ground in West Papua, as the Indonesians moved in their forces under UN administration, contemporary reports revealed a glimpse of what the Papuan population would face under Indonesian rule. McKinlay King quotes a United Nations Temporary Executive Authority report from Divisional Commander G.S. Rawlings, dated 12 December 1962:

> The Indonesians strike me as out to attain their ends quite ruthlessly if necessary. They brook no serious discussion of facts or ideas contrary to their doctrinaire beliefs. In fact, in this they are very like the Japanese before the war. It cannot be long before they get themselves most intensely hated ... By far the majority of the Papuans in my Division dread the consequence of the Indonesian invasion and it would take little to influence some of them to resist, whether it would do them any good or not.[2]

The arrests of Papuans who spoke out against the Indonesians began. The Papuan volunteer auxiliaries formed under the Dutch started clashing with Indonesian soldiers. In one instance they stormed an Indonesian armoury and acquired ammunition and more than 1000 weapons.

The incidents continued, and as the UN observers and their Pakistani troops began to withdraw, it was clear the Papuans were now on their own. By 1 May 1963, when the Indonesians officially took over the administration, there were no UN officials in the territory. The Indonesians had brought in thirty warships and twenty aeroplanes for the occasion. Although Papua was still technically in a transitional phase, the Indonesian administrators and troops quickly made their presence felt.

With no UN presence, McKinlay King notes, and no other international observers, 'the Indonesian military was unrestrained'. A declassified report by US diplomat Frank Galbraith reads:

> Perhaps the most oft-cited grievance of the Irianese is that the Indonesians cleaned out the shops and storehouses in the period immediately following their takeover of West Irian administration in 1963. Missionaries reported that they had witnessed Indonesian military personnel loading up Air Force planes at night with goods taken from local merchants. Within months of Indonesian takeover on May 1 1963, there was an acute shortage of food and consumer goods.[3]

Comment from Australia, the Netherlands and the United States was limited. The takeover was effectively complete and the Indonesians began making plans to exploit the natural resources of their new territory. The rights of the locals were at best ignored and at worst abused and violated. West Papua had gone from a colonial backwater preparing for independence in the 1950s to a war zone and then to an occupied country in the space of three years. The local people had not been consulted and had repeatedly shown their opposition through petitions, acts of peaceful resistance and sometimes violence, often initiated by the incoming Indonesian forces. In 1969 the UN-sponsored 'Act of Free Choice' saw 1026 of their fellow citizens forced under threat to vote for integration into Indonesia. They were representatives of the almost 1 million Papuans living in the territory at the time. The West Papuans had been abandoned by the international community.

*

The Indonesian nation that incorporated Papua in 1963 was about to go through some tumultuous changes. Emboldened by his diplomatic success in acquiring West Papua, President Sukarno continued to play the United States off against the Soviets. He flirted with both and thought he could get away with it. The United States, though supportive of Sukarno, became increasingly concerned about his links to the Soviet bloc. As the American leadership became more involved in South-East Asia due to the conflict in Vietnam, they began to fear the region's largest communist party, the Indonesian PKI (Partai Komunis Indonesia).

In 1965 the Americans, working through their military links to the Indonesian military, switched allegiance to General Suharto. He staged what was in effect a coup against Sukarno, on the pretence of restoring security. With full US backing – and, as a consequence, Australia's – Suharto's regime was encouraged to destroy the PKI. The CIA even handed over extensive lists of communist or leftist supporters and organisations, such as trade unions, to be targeted and wiped out. Under Suharto, the army and its nationalist supporters swept through the country, killing and imprisoning anywhere between 500,000 and 3 million people (accounts vary). It was a huge bloodletting that continues to traumatise survivors and stigmatise their families today. Indonesia's current president, Joko Widodo – known as Jokowi – promised at last to address the issue, but survivors and their descendants still gather in Jakarta outside the government palace every Thursday demanding redress and recognition.

West Papua became a place of exile for some of those leaders and individuals spared death. A camp was established in the remote area of Tanah Merah, in the wilderness north of Merauke, and many dissidents, or those accused of being dissidents, were sent there.

More than a purge, Suharto's anti-communist campaign was a wave of localised massacres supported, encouraged and carried out by the army. When it was all over, Suharto was emboldened by the United States' firm support. Over the next decade, he continued to see threats in Aceh, whose people had never stopped resisting the central authority, just as they had never accepted Dutch rule before that. Suharto clamped down on their insurgency and facilitated the establishment of a massive ExxonMobil gas facility near the city of Lhokseumawe, stirring up resistance to Jakarta's rule there. Then, in 1975, he invaded the former Portuguese colony of East Timor. Both operations were sanctioned by the United States.

It was in the mid-1970s that Suharto's attention moved back to West Papua. Confident he would not be opposed by the United States, the United Nations or neighbours like Australia or by-then independent Papua New Guinea, he increased operations there. This involved aerial bombing, and helicopters and troops on the ground going into areas that had never seen Indonesians at all. In some of the highland areas this brutality was the first contact with the outside world, aside from a few missionaries and the occasional Dutch exploratory mission in the 1930s, both of which had been relatively benign. But the Indonesians had honed their tactics in the invasion of East Timor in 1975 and its bloody aftermath, when they bombed, strafed and pursued the Timorese who had fled to the hills.

Well armed with US military equipment, much of it Vietnam War–era surplus (the legacy of Indonesia's willing participation in the Vietnam War), the Indonesians now bombed and strafed villages in the highlands. This led to a massive movement of the population, who were unarmed and had no recourse other than to flee, both across the border to PNG and to other districts. That resulted in further problems: people died from starvation and disease during the long walk across the mountains, and when they arrived in the PNG camps there was little relief. Living in remote, sparsely populated equatorial jungle along the border – in some cases in clearings bulldozed to accommodate them – they were largely left to fend for themselves. Foreign aid was limited. There was a reason not many people lived in the areas they were settled in: the land was not very fertile, and the refugees faced severe shortages in food, medical aid and any kind of help from a world too scared of Indonesia even to acknowledge their existence. Surrounded by thick jungle and mountains, and sometimes hostile locals, the refugees were not going anywhere.

The late 1970s were a time of intense Indonesian military operations, and it was in this period that the majority of Papuan deaths occurred. In an article for *The Conversation*, theologian, social anthropologist and activist Benny Giay listed the operations that contributed to a Papuan death toll of somewhere between 100,000 and 500,000, depending on which account you read: 'Sadar Operation (1962, 1965–67), Wisnumurti Operation (1963), Wibawa Operation (1969), Pamungkas Operation (1970–71), military operations in Jayawijaya (1977–80), Sapu Bersih Operation (1979–82), and Tumpas Operation (1983–84) are only a few of a series of violent acts of oppression that have confronted ordinary Papuans,' he wrote in 2016.

> Today, Indonesia's militaristic approach in West Papua remains intact. This approach has resulted in a series of acts of intimidation and terror committed by

> security forces. They are involved in land expropriation and natural resources extraction under the banner of development and investment, in the name of Papuan welfare.[4]

The Indonesians had carte blanche to do what they wanted in West Papua. So they tried to suppress and depopulate the areas where they saw economic opportunity. The operation in Jayawijaya from 1977 to 1980 is a case in point. After an OPM attack on the Grasberg mine in 1977, the Indonesians launched a huge operation to clear the mountain villages anywhere near the mine. I spoke to survivors of that operation in one of the border camps just inside PNG in 2002. They told me about the helicopters, the planes, the ground troops coming in. Things they had never seen before. The brutality of the Indonesian troops who followed through, burning down villages, shooting, raping, stealing anything of value. The OV-10 Bronco aircraft and Bell 'Huey' helicopters they flew in on, the M16s they carried – even the helmets they wore – were US-issue. The Papuans fled hundreds of kilometres on foot on trails through the mountains to PNG, where they remain to this day.

*

That stage of the war in West Papua went mostly unreported and ignored by the outside world, despite the herculean work of a few journalists. There was a lack of access to the area and, as they say, nobody of influence had skin in the game. The people of PNG, though largely sympathetic to the plight of their fellow Melanesians across the arbitrary border, had their hands tied by their financial reliance on Australia, which was advising them to stay out of it. Both major Australian political parties were unquestioningly following the Indonesian line. As in East Timor, the people calling for action in West Papua comprised an unlikely coalition of left-wing activists and Catholic and Baptist missionaries. They were marginalised and derided, and their reports discredited. Virtually no one covered it and as a result there was no competitive imperative for news organisations to cover it.

There was another reason for the media silence, too: the lingering memory of the Balibo Five – the Australian journalists killed in cold blood in the border town of Balibo as the Indonesians prepared to invade, and the execution of a sixth at the wharf in Dili on the first day of the invasion. The ruthlessness of those killings, the utter disregard of any international norms and the spineless and reprehensible cover-up of the circumstances of their deaths by both the Indonesian and the Australian governments had spooked the journalists and media organisations. If the Indonesians said you couldn't go to an area, you didn't go; the assumption was they would kill you and no one would intervene. That same attitude prevailed in the mid-1990s, when I started reporting in Indonesia. There was that unspoken example in the backs of reporters' and editors' minds. They wouldn't ask you to go to a restricted or militarised area. But if you did go and came back with a good story, they would run it. You were on your own.

Eventually, in the 1980s and '90s, writers such as George Monbiot ventured into the areas cleared out by the Indonesians. Robin Osborne also produced a landmark account of that time. Filmmaker Mark Worth, photojournalist Ben Bohane and ABC-then-SBS reporter Mark Davis continued to try to cover the events in West Papua. Lindsay Murdoch of Fairfax provided excellent coverage of the massacre on the island of Biak, off the north coast of Papua. As in East Timor, the demise of the Suharto regime in May 1998 led to a period of confusion among the Indonesian military commanders on the ground. They didn't know if they could expel, arrest or kill journalists and protesters as they had in the past, and it created an environment where it was finally possible for reporters to get to previously inaccessible places and speak to people. The turmoil in Jakarta had created a kind of stasis among the military commanders in the far-flung provinces. But they were watching. In short, they had lifted the lid off dissent enough for those who supported Papuan independence to show themselves. They collected names, identified activists, photographed them. Drew up their lists of who to kill or arrest, and waited for the political winds to change.

The Indonesian military was far from idle throughout the 1990s. In 2004 the UN Refugee Agency published a list detailing the reported killings, demonstrations and riots caused by Indonesian responses to a slowly re-empowered movement for independence between 1990 and 2000.[5] These were the incidents *reported* throughout that period; many, many more acts of casual violence and intimidation were also carried out.

In fact, the list is quite conservative, in both figures of dead Papuans and the level of violence. Access to Papua was still restricted, and foreigners still heavily monitored and harassed by being followed, threatened and told outright they would be killed if they went here or there or spoke to certain people. For Papuans it had become a way of life: constant intimidation and violence and extortion by the Indonesian military, punctuated by short, sharp moments of protest and resistance, followed by the inevitable crackdown.

It was an endless cycle of violence that the Indonesians thought they could shoot, torture, arrest and strangle their way out of. As I had found in East Timor, in order to get a story run you had to have more than ten dead; the daily grind of one shot there, one beating there, one arrest there, never made it into the press. I'll never forget the cynical words delivered down the phone by one Australian editor after I had watched a man – a boy, really – shot dead in front of my eyes as I cowered in a ditch to avoid Indonesian gunfire in East Timor. 'So what are your plucky brown fellows up to today?' he said. He didn't run the story. The daily oppressive reality that the local population faced in Papua, and continue to face, was not news in the international forum. But it was that daily fear, and the casual violence and intimidation, that was the story.

*

The cosy relationship between Indonesia and Australia was tested in January 2006, when forty-three Papuan asylum seekers turned up in a traditional outrigger boat on Cape York in Queensland. They said they were fleeing government violence and the 'genocide' against their people by the Indonesian authorities. It had taken them five days to get there from the southern coast of Papua. The Australian government, under Prime Minister John Howard and Minister for Foreign Affairs Alexander Downer, didn't know what to do with them, so they sent them all the way across the country to Australia's remote warehouse for refugees on Christmas Island, in the Indian Ocean, off Western Australia. They held them there until late March when, having found no reason to detain them further, they granted all but one a temporary visa.

Indonesia was angry at the decision and issued the usual statements, saying there were no human rights abuses occurring in West Papua. Meanwhile, twenty-two students were seriously wounded at a rally in Timika opposing the Grasberg mine and the environmental degradation it caused. The Indonesian police who carried out that shooting were actually temporarily disarmed by their comrades and confined to barracks. The information about the shootings came from the church. The Indonesians responded by floating the idea that not just journalists but perhaps all foreigners should be banned from West Papua. In February 2010, Indonesia's then minister of defence, Juwono Sudarsono, gave his reasons for maintaining restrictions on foreign media reporting from Papua: 'We feel that our unity and cohesion are being threatened by the presence of foreign intrusion and concerns so there is a balance between international concerns and sovereignty that we want to strike very peacefully.' Minister Sudarsono also stated that the restrictions should extend to foreign NGOs and churches which 'might create conflict in the province by encouraging Papuans to campaign on issues of human rights', according to Human Rights Watch. He said he feared reporters could be 'used as a platform'.[6]

I remember reading that line in *The Straits Times*, sitting in a restaurant in Singapore with an old journalist friend who had covered Indonesia for many years. We laughed at the sheer idiocy of the statement. What if we were allowed to go to West Papua, which we hadn't been since 2003? Would we encourage people to dissent simply by listening to and recording their stories of mistreatment by the Indonesian military? It was as if the whole situation of Indonesian police and military, intelligence agents and their sponsored militias killing, abducting, jailing and torturing the local Papuans would just disappear if there were no foreigners there. No journalists, no NGOs providing humanitarian aid and no churches, which, the Indonesian government implied, were stirring up the trouble. The way the Indonesians saw it, or at least pretended to see it, the 50,000-plus Indonesian troops and police and their actions were not the problem; it was the pesky foreigners who caused all of this.

Such bad faith was just a way for the military to maintain its position, making money from kickbacks from logging, mining and plantations in Papua. Money to pay for security from what was initially a minimal threat. Over the years it became a bigger threat as the Papuan people became fed up with the corrupt 'autonomy' programs of the early 2000s, which enriched a few and gave nothing to the rest. All they could see around their region was development that did not benefit them; in fact, it displaced and disregarded them. A few well-positioned Papuans made some money, but it mostly went to Indonesian companies or individuals, many associated with the Indonesian military, which had created and maintained the conditions to carry out what amounted to a shakedown of the resources of Papua. That is why the road, the Trans-Papua Highway, became a symbol for both sides. For the Indonesians it was a symbol of success and development, something to be celebrated. For the Papuans it was like a spear through the heart, killing their traditional life and claims on the land.

Jokowi, despite being supported by an overwhelming majority in Papua at the election of 2014, has done nothing in the time since. Six years later, the random killings, endless arrests and egregious torture continue. One recent video shows a Papuan man being bound then sliced with a large military knife as Indonesian troops stand around laughing. Another shows a Papuan man restrained in a cell as Indonesian soldiers throw in a snake and take pictures of his terror. This material leaks out because Indonesians post it on social media. They seem to revel in the cruelty they can inflict on the Papuan people. In some bizarre form of bragging or machismo, these Indonesian soldiers and police feel the need to publish and share this constant drip-feed of appalling abuses. Is it some kind of warning to Papuans not to support independence, or just a symptom of the moral vacuum they enter once they are deployed to Papua? I don't know the answer, but I do know one thing: the Indonesians deride the Papuans, demean them and treat them very harshly, but at the root of that derision is a deep fear. They are fundamentally scared of the Papuans. Despite the Indonesians having been there for more than fifty years, West Papua and its people are still very foreign to them. They have tried to create a society that is a mirror image of their own in a land they occupied against the wishes of the local population, and the local people have never forgotten or forgiven that take-over. To my mind, they never will.

West Papuan men scale a cliff in the central highlands of Papua on their way to Papua New Guinea in 2019. There are no roads through the area, which hosts some of the highest mountains in Asia.

West Papuan men use a jungle trail to flee Indonesian forces as they seek shelter further in the mountains in 2019.

GOLD, COPPER, GAS

The importance of the Grasberg mine – symbolically and financially – for both the Indonesians and the Papuans cannot be overstated. The high-grade copper and gold ore of Mount Carstensz, the highest peak in Oceania, was discovered by an expedition to scale the mountain in 1936. It wasn't until 1960 that the extent of the deposit was discovered by representatives of the small US-based mining company Freeport-McMoRan. They cajoled and lobbied the Indonesian government into granting them a licence to further explore the deposit, even though Indonesia did not yet have official control of the Dutch colony. But the little-known company read the way the wind was blowing. They got their deal formalised in 1963, and President Suharto awarded the contract two years before the Indonesians formally seized full control of the colony with the Act of Free Choice in 1969.

This was the first major foreign investment contract to be signed by the Suharto regime. It gave the company the right to seize land with no compensation to those who lived on or owned it. The Indonesian military and police simply began by relocating the Amungme and Komoro peoples who lived in the huge area set aside for the mine down to Timika, on the coast. There they suffered starvation and diseases they had never known on the mountain.

Timika is now a busy, dusty, oppressive place. Despite sitting on the edge of a vast wilderness, it has a dead river and is dominated by the mine. There are a lot of Indonesians in Timika. They have come over the years to search for work in the mine or in businesses that feed off it. There are grubby brothels and bars run out of weathered, dilapidated timber shacks. The market is covered with grey dust. Buses and trucks from the mine speed through town.

The massive Grasberg mine went on to earn annual turnovers of around US$2 billion: it was basically a mountain of gold and copper, and the wealth was divided between Freeport-McMoRan and the Indonesians. Freeport became the highest foreign taxpayer to the central government. The Papuan people got nothing. The Indonesian military and police helped with the establishment and protection of the mine's operation, and in turn received kickbacks, bonuses and annual payments in excess of tens of millions of dollars, delivered by the company annually. The autonomy laws pushed through by the Indonesians promised Timika a larger share of the taxation revenue from the mine. But by all accounts that has failed to materialise.

The first human rights abuses by Indonesian troops in the areas surrounding the mine were reported in 1972. Resentment was growing and the locals were fighting back. In 1977, the OPM men under Kelly Kwalik attacked and managed to briefly halt operations of the mine's slurry line, which carried the ore down to the coast. The response was a huge Indonesian military operation, killing at least 800 Papuans and scattering thousands more into the mountains.

Freeport funds – then as now – a large part of the military activity in the vicinity of the mine and further afield. It pays for 'guard houses and guard posts, barracks, parade grounds and ammunition storage facilities', according to a 2002 report by the US-based Robert F. Kennedy Memorial Center for Human Rights.[7] The report quotes a former helicopter pilot who worked at the mine saying how common it was in the 1970s and '80s for Freeport helicopters to transport Indonesian military troops on operations against civilians. It features detailed accounts of torture and beatings carried out in Freeport shipping containers in 1994 and 1995, documented by the Catholic Church.

Later, the relationship between the mine, the military and the local police became murkier still. On 31 August 2002, a group from the international school that educated the children of the Freeport mine workers in the enclave town of Tembagapura, an American-built suburb in the jungle, was returning from a picnic. On a section of mountain road with a steep fall on one side and a hill on the other, armed men sprayed their vehicles with bullets. Two American teachers were killed, along with the school's Indonesian principal. Eight Americans were also wounded.

Although initially the OPM was blamed for the attack and the military rounded up the usual suspects among the Papuans, it quickly became apparent it was the military itself that was responsible. Those assigned to protect the Freeport workers had turned on them in an apparent extortion attempt to reinstate benefits, such as free flights in and out of Timika, financial bonuses and other perks previously enjoyed by the troops assigned to protect the mine and the nearby housing settlement. The investigation to find out who was responsible for the killings was carried out by the Indonesian police but was also monitored and assisted by US diplomats and the FBI. According to *The New York Times*, 'Suspicion quickly turned away from the separatists. In the course of that early investigation, the Australian government gave the United States a telephone intercept between Indonesian military commanders. The conversation, which took place after the incident, leaves no doubt of military involvement in the killings.'[8] The article continued: '"Extortion, pure and simple," said a Western intelligence analyst, explaining what he believed was behind the attack. Freeport has declined to answer any questions about the killings or about payments to the police and the military.'

The case was 'resolved' in 2007 with the jailing of the Papuans who were said to be responsible for the shooting. The Papuans pleaded their innocence and there were demonstrations outside the court. No Indonesian military officers were charged.

As well as paying massive taxes to the central government in Jakarta, Freeport-McMoRan and BP, which runs extensive operations at the Tangguh gas field in West Papua, influence their own governments to wilfully ignore the reality of a people reduced to second-class and expendable citizens, and in some cases criminals and enemies, in their own land.

In December 2018, Freeport sold or gifted 51 per cent of its shares in the mine to Indonesian state-owned companies and individuals, among them former generals. As the deal was finalised, Joko Widodo hailed it as a victory for Indonesia. He promised to send some 10 per cent of the government's profit from the mine to Papua for development.

But the offloading of shares has also reduced the company's responsibility for the massive environmental damage it has caused. The tailings in the local waterways run all the way past Timika, down to the sea. I saw the dead river when I was there in 2003: it was a mass of grey sludge the local people avoided. Papuan activists said people could no longer fish in the river or drink the water as it made them sick. Nothing has been done about this, by either the mine or the authorities, and with the nominal transfer of responsibility to the Indonesian government, action seems even more unlikely.

*

On 7 March 2020, an Associated Press report was published in *The Washington Post*. It detailed renewed fighting in the villages near the mine and the company town of Tembagapura. There had been a week-long shootout between independence fighters and the security guarding the mine, leading the Indonesian authorities to forcibly evacuate the surrounding villages, bussing out at least 2000 civilians. The Indonesian police chief was quoted as saying the OPM had started the violence on

29 February with an attack on a police post that killed one police officer and wounded two others. The report quoted a local National Liberation Army of West Papua commander, Lekagak Telenggen, claiming responsibility for the attacks: 'We will keep fighting until PT Freeport Indonesia stops operating and closes,' he said.[9]

Three days later, Benny Wenda issued this letter to the international community:

> As the world faces the coronavirus crisis, my people face a renewed humanitarian crisis in West Papua. From Puncak Jaya to Intan Jaya, Nduga to Timika, over 45,000 have been displaced by Indonesian military operations since December 2018. As you read this, the Indonesia military is mobilising to protect the world's largest gold and third-largest copper mine, Grasberg, run by US company Freeport McMoRan. Thousands, including entire villages near the mine, are fleeing.
>
> Indonesia is cynically using the coronavirus to conceal its operations, banning all foreigners from West Papua as it begins depopulating villages. If Indonesia wants to protect us from the virus, why is it forcing women and children into the forest, at risk of dying from lack of food and medicine? Clearly, Indonesia wants to prevent any international observers from witnessing its latest massacres.
>
> Indonesia has deployed 700 new troops in West Papua this year alone, on top of an additional 16,000 last year.

This doesn't include the newly-deployed Brimob police officers or intelligence sections. We have been peacefully demanding our right to self-determination – Indonesia has been sending in heavily armed troops. The purpose is clear: to eliminate West Papuans and crush all signs of resistance. The 57 political prisoners incarcerated since the August 2019 uprising demonstrate Indonesia's true intentions.

One way Indonesia is doing this is by trying to stigmatise the West Papuan military wing, the West Papua Army. Indonesia tries to smear the West Papua Army and ULMWP [United Liberation Movement for West Papua] as separatists or an Armed Criminal Group (KKB). Does a KKB sit at the table internationally, with 79 heads of state in the African, Caribbean and Pacific Group? Does a KKB sit with the Indonesian government at the Melanesian Spearhead Group? In 1961, we were already recognised as the state-in-waiting of West Papua. Indonesia hijacked our independence and destroyed our sovereignty. Today, we are fighting to reclaim our sovereignty. These are not the actions of an 'Armed Criminal Group'.

There have always been West Papuans who, with the support of the people, defend themselves, their mountains and their forests. They are the West Papuan home guard. Indonesia uses the existence of the West Papua Army to bomb villages, kill civilians and arrest non-violent activists. The world should not be fooled by this.

The people of West Papua have lived on their lands for tens of thousands of years. Until Indonesia came there was no mass killing, deforestation or pollution. Now, our land is a hunting ground for the Indonesian military.

Every country has the right to defend its ancestral lands against an invader. The West Papua Army seeks to reclaim its land from an illegal occupier. If we went to Java and tried to steal Indonesia's land, we would expect the Indonesian military to resist. Indonesia came to our country, illegally, in 1963, and has killed 500,000 Papuan men, women and children since. We have lost everything. Is it any surprise then, that West Papuans' united self-defence army seeks to resist this genocide, to ensure the survival of our people?

We do not accept the presence of the Indonesian military or multinational corporations on our soil. All the international solidarity networks must mobilise to defend us now. The people of West Papua are fighting with their lives every day to defend our forests, mountains and rivers. We are ground zero in the fight to protect our global natural environment.

As the West Papua Army defends its people and its environment, the Indonesian military mobilises to defend Freeport McMoRan and its huge environmentally destructive gold and copper mine. Freeport is at the root of the West Papua genocide. The company has been operating in the middle of a genocide, and providing direct and indirect support to the Indonesian police and military to carry out mass killings. Freeport has long been the single largest tax payer to the Indonesian colonial

State, taxes which are used to buy the weapons which kill my people. It is the same story as the genocide in East Timor. The depopulation of the villages around the mine right now is a continuation of this bloody history. We demand that Freeport stop operating in West Papua until the bloodshed ceases.[10]

*

Another factor underlying the renewed military activity in the mine region is the road. The Trans-Papua Highway is due to come to that area in 2020. The Indonesian military is now in control of the road's construction, and from its perspective, clearing the villages in the vicinity of the mine makes perverse sense: if you take all the civilians away, you cannot be accused of killing or mistreating them. Anyone who is left can then be labelled a combatant and killed on sight. And that allows the Indonesian shareholders, who now own 51 per cent of the massive mine, to profit until the mine is exhausted and the environmental degradation complete. Maybe then they will allow the local people back onto their denuded and polluted land.

Papuan men carry a wounded or sick colleague across a river as they flee in 2019, trying to find safety from Indonesian military operations.

On 20 September 2019, the Indonesian army shot dead five citizens from Iniye village, Mbua district, Nduga, who were taking food to the refugees.

Whole villages of men, women and children have fled into the mountains. Estimates of 45,000 people fleeing from Nduga alone were repeatedly reported in late 2019.

Families join the widespread movement of people fleeing the violence across the mountains in 2019.

RAISING THE FLAG

A road through the highlands of West Papua was an ambitious idea. It would link the major population centres of Jayapura, the capital on the north coast; Sorong, the gas-rich eastern centre; and, significantly, the highland town of Wamena and the gold- and copper-rich area around Timika. It would extend all the way south to Merauke. The road, in theory, would bring wealth, development and prosperity to previously isolated areas. But as the Papuans saw it, the road would in reality bring military occupation by Indonesian troops, exploitation by foreign companies, environmental destruction and colonisation by Indonesian transmigrants. The road would bring the death of their centuries-old way of life, previously undisturbed aside from the occasional Indonesian military incursion and the mostly welcome arrival of Christian missionaries. It was inevitable, really, that the plan by the Indonesian state to develop the isolated interior of the West Papua and Papua provinces would meet resistance.

The Nduga area, in the mountains and virgin rainforest to the north of Timika, had long been an isolated stronghold of independence supporters. They grew sweet potato, raised pigs, lived mostly off the land. Their lives were simple but had been punctuated by Indonesian military operations throughout the 1970s, '80s and '90s, when there had been large movements of the population fleeing to neighbouring provinces and across the border to Papua New Guinea.

Isolated in the highlands, many of the Dani and Nduga people had never seen Indonesians or any foreigners before the 1970s. They didn't know they were under Indonesian rule. They vaguely recalled the Dutch, but that had been limited to a few expeditions and no attempts to impose colonial rule. They had just been left alone with their agriculture and self-sustaining lifestyle that had evolved since their island was formed with the break-up of Gondwanaland, way back at the start of time. They hadn't migrated there. They were just simply there.

For centuries they had fought regular tribal wars against each other and any other outsiders, conducted in a ritual, almost ceremonial way. The fighters from both sides would gather in an open space at a specified time. Each side would send its best fighters into the field. Arrows and spears would soon solve the dispute – sometimes it was about land, sometimes it was about a woman, or sometimes even something as small as a pig. Usually only a few of the warriors would be killed until it was called off and a truce was reached between the tribes. When observed by anthropologists in the 1960s, it was documented as a very formal and ritualised approach to conflict that resulted in a mutually agreed outcome, and then everyone would go back to their villages and fields. But unfortunately for the Nduga and the Dani, when the Indonesian troops finally arrived in the highlands in the 1970s, they brought troops and aircraft that did not play by these rules.

*

The local OPM leaders in the 1990s were Kelly Kwalik, Daniel Kogoya and Silas Kogoya. They presided over the kidnapping of twenty-six hostages from the village of Mapenduma in the highlands on 8 January 1996. The hostages comprised twenty Indonesians, four Britons and two Dutch – including a pregnant woman – all part of a World Wildlife Fund mission conducting biodiversity research. Things ended badly, with the Indonesian military using a Red Cross helicopter to fly in soldiers, including foreign mercenaries, to save the captives and open fire on the independence fighters after a truce had been arranged. The independence fighters acted in good faith for the safety of the hostages; the Indonesians did not.

Australian reporter Mark Davis pursued that story for the ABC's *Four Corners* and found many holes and discrepancies in the official account. His investigations led him to conclude that both the Indonesian and British militaries had been involved in the operation to release the hostages by posing as the International Committee of the Red Cross (ICRC), which had developed a rapport with the hostage-takers. According to Davis, they used the same white chartered helicopter used by the ICRC to gain access to the village where the hostages were being held. They landed surrounded by locals who trusted the ICRC. They then got out, assumed firing positions and began to shoot into the gathered crowd of villagers. It was well documented in his Walkley Award–winning report 'Blood on the Cross', which aired in 1999.

Davis wrote to me in December 2018:

> In 1999 I got into the Southern Highlands of West Papua, one of the remotest parts of the world, to interview independence leader Kelly Kwalik and his commanders Daniel Kogoya and Silas Kogoya … In 1977, after a West Papuan flag was raised in the highlands, the Indonesian airforce launched a full-scale attack on the highlands. The valleys were carpet bombed. Thousands were killed. Many fled never to return and remained with Kwalik in the forest.
>
> Silas Kogoya sang me a song which narrated the history of his people from the time of the 1977 bombing. It tells a story of being hunted from the air for twenty years, including the 1996 attacks from helicopters flying the Red Cross flag (with the complicity of the ICRC …). Silas's song is an oral history and a warning to his young people about the dangers they face from the air. His wife had a baby son that year.
>
> A few weeks ago I heard reports of more gunship attacks in the Southern Highlands. Silas's son, now nineteen, was one of those killed. His entire life would have been spent being hunted like a beast and ended as his father predicted.[11]

The song, which Silas sings directly to the camera in Mark's report, is moving in its simplicity and tragedy. At the time it was recorded, Silas's son would have been an infant.

'Oh mother, I'm going to die,' the song goes. 'Oh mother, I'm going to die. We are going to die. We are going to die. Be careful or the Javanese will bomb you. Hit by an atom bomb and we die. Hit by an atom bomb and we die.'[12]

When the people in Nduga felt threatened in 2018, it was to Egianus, the youngest surviving son of Silas, that they turned.

*

On 1 December 2018 it began in a remote highland village in the Nduga region of the central highlands. As they had done every year since 1961, the local people gathered to raise the Morning Star flag. Speeches were made and dancing and singing took place. It was a peaceful event but the intent was clear: the people wanted independence. Raising the flag had become a ritual act of defiance by the people of West Papua. Sometimes they were shot by Indonesian security forces, sometimes they were arrested, sometimes they were simply beaten and the flag torn down. Occasionally the demonstrations were tolerated, and ended peaceably. But officially, under Indonesian law, it was and is still illegal to raise the flag.

Usually the flag-raising goes unnoticed in this isolated place. But the road has come to town. The Indonesians are building a bridge outside the village, pushing the road through to Wamena. It has taken them years, since the 1990s, to get this far. Publicly they are saying they will complete it in the next year.

Some of the Indonesian roadworkers come into the village from the nearby work camp. Somebody notices some of the roadworkers taking photos of the flag-raising with their phones. Panic runs through the crowd. If they are identified participating in the ceremony, they could be arrested, tortured and even killed. It has happened before. They turn on the Indonesians, who run back to their accommodation. The locals gather the boys. They believe the workers are actually Indonesian military posing as roadworkers. The person they go to is the son of the local leader Silas Kogoya. Egianus. He has the guns and the men he needs. He goes to the Indonesian roadworkers' accommodation and rounds them up at gunpoint, including an Indonesian soldier. He and his men march them out into the bush. They shoot them dead. They deem the threat to their community worth more than the Indonesians' lives. This time they could do it; in the past it had always been the other way round. And the past has been their entire lives.

The figures of Indonesian dead are disputed. Initially Egianus says they killed more than thirty. They are proud of their actions and send out photos of heavily armed OPM fighters posing with modern weaponry: M16s with grenade launchers, FNCs, even Steyr copies, all made under licence in Surabaya by weapons manufacturer PT Pindad and no doubt acquired there by cashed-up West Papuans. The Indonesians say nineteen roadworkers and one Indonesian soldier have been killed. They add that the construction of the bridge and the road will be taken over by the army. They deploy 2000 Indonesian soldiers, helicopters and a further 650 commandos to continue the operation. It is the helicopters that are the worst. They are used as platforms to shoot or drop white phosphorous grenades or bomblets that inflict horrible injuries on the populace.

As Mark Davis and I reported in *The Saturday Paper* in December 2018, we received an overwhelming number of images of Papuans wounded from the conflict zone in Nduga as the Indonesian military carried out reprisals against the civilian population:

> There are burns around the wounds. The flesh appears to have been torn open or burrowed into, the victims' clothing melted or cut away. At least seven are dead. Thousands more have fled into the hills.
>
> These are the first images of a major operation being conducted by the Indonesian military in the central highlands of West Papua. Other photographs show yellow-tipped bombs, collected by villagers. Some weapons appear to be white phosphorus, banned under international law for use of this kind.
>
> White phosphorus is considered both an incendiary weapon and a chemical weapon. It burns through skin and flesh, down to the bone. It cannot be extinguished. The only way to save a person hit with it is to submerge them in water and attempt to remove the phosphorus.

> Many die from internal burns. Others from the phosphorous absorbed into their bodies, which can cause multiple organ failure.
>
> A military source confirms the weapons 'appear to be incendiary or white phosphorus'. The source says 'even the smallest specks burn through clothing, skin, down to the bone and keep on bubbling away'.[13]

Many of the images are so graphic they are unpublishable. Soon after the story runs, it becomes very hard for the people in Nduga to get mobile or internet signal sufficient to send images. That remains the case at the time of writing. The Indonesians have presumably cut the signal.

The photos of the wounds are enough to prompt the United Nations commissioner for human rights, Michelle Bachelet, to demand UN access to the area to investigate an internationally recognised violation of the laws of war. The Indonesians, led by the 'centrist' Widodo, at first say yes. But then they say no. The former generals in the government and the active generals in the Indonesian military are not going to allow it. They say no UN mission, no foreign journalists, no foreign organisations whatsoever can enter the province of Nduga. The local people remember the last big Indonesian operations in their mountains and valleys, in the 1970s, 1980s and into the early '90s, which involved bombing, the burning of villages, the killing of those they encountered and widespread looting and rape. The villagers back then soon learnt how to flee into the jungles and the mountains.

And that is what they do now. Thirty-seven thousand local inhabitants flee, mostly by foot. There are precious few roads in Nduga, and they know that to escape from there they have to walk through jungle and across the high, snow-covered passes. Just under 200, mostly women and children, have been reported dead. Many, many more are unaccounted for, hiding in the jungle or dead. The numbers reportedly fleeing have since risen to more than 45,000, and 238 are confirmed dead from the hardship, sickness and starvation, but the true number of dead is sure to be much higher, as many of the groups are isolated and unlikely to contact any authority on any account. There was one small story I read about a Papuan man trying to return to Nduga on the highway carrying some food. He was shot dead by the Indonesian forces protecting the road. Some of the displaced have fled deeper into rugged mountains and jungle that they hope will protect them. Others have opted to go to the highlands centre of Wamena. Some are fleeing across the border after a long trek through the mountains to Papua New Guinea.

The extraordinary figure of 45,000 displaced people originally came from the church groups in or near the Nduga region that have been trying organise some sort of aid. It has been reported widely and is a calculation based on the previous populations of the villages that are now deserted. Pacific Media Watch assessed media reports from the region and had their own team of four journalists investigating, as well as local reporters on the ground. They published a piece on 21 January 2020 confirming the figure of 45,000 internally displaced people.[14] Reports from

Papua New Guinea sources such as the Port Moresby-based daily *Post Courier* have also reported a steady trickle amounting to thousands of displaced people from Nduga arriving in the heavily forested, mountainous and remote border regions.

*

After our *Saturday Paper* article was published, the former Indonesian general Wiranto, the coordinating minister for political, judicial and security affairs, sent the paper an extraordinary denial:

> Dear Sir,
>
> In an age of hoax and false news, it is indeed a sorrowful day to witness that the *Saturday Paper* have fallen into a similar trapping such as reflected by the recent article 'Chemical weapons dropped on Papua' written by John Martinkus and Mark Davis.
>
> Following the execution of 19 harmless construction workers in Nduga on 4 December 2018, who were there to build the Trans-Papua highway to elevate the well-being of Papuans as Indonesian citizens, the Indonesian Government have indeed conducted security measures in Nduga on 4–15 December 2018.
>
> Such measures were intended to curtail the presence of the armed separatist group, which have conducted heinous crimes such as kidnapping, torture, and summary execution of innocent civilians, including local villagers,

including local civilians as well as Indonesian police and soldiers. To this day, at least 4 more innocent construction workers are still held by these criminals.

The law enforcement operation was conducted in accordance with the prevailing norms and in line with the existing regulations and procedures.

The involvement of the military component in the operation, most particularly air wing rotary assets, was strictly as assistance to law enforcement officials, and not a military deployment per se in an otherwise internal security operation.

While Mr Martinkus and Mr Davis have explained the circumstances of the said incident in their article, yet the two writers have indeed failed to implement the principle of 'cover both sides' concerning the use of chemical weapons by the Indonesian Government.

The allegations are baseless, non-factual and misleading.

Had Mr Martinkus and Mr Davis taken the time to request clarification from the Indonesian Government, they might have known that Indonesia is a compliant member of the Organisation for the Prohibition of Chemical Weapons (OPCW).

As such, Indonesia has no possession of any chemical agents as listed in Schedule 1 of Chemical Weapons Convention. Accordingly, Indonesia also imports, uses and stores Schedules 2 and 3 chemical agents for strictly peaceful purposes in supporting national industry. Such have been confirmed by at least 19 OPCW inspections since 2004 until this day. Messrs Martinkus and Davis would also have discovered that Indonesia's Coordinating Minister for Political, Security and Law Wiranto have stated on 17 December 2018 at a press conference that the allegations of the use of chemical weapons such as white phosphorus munition is false and baseless.

In the regard, the two writers apparently have been ensnared by the hoax and false news as have been propagated many times before by the supporters of Papuan separatist group.

Through this letter we implore the *Saturday Paper* to retract the said article and issue a public apology to maintain its journalistic credibility. We would also like to have this letter published in your distinguished periodical as our right of reply.

We urge you to advise Mr Martinkus and Mr Davis that their inaccurate and questionable have undoubtedly endangered the fine reputation of the *Saturday Paper*. We also urge both Mr Martinkus and Mr Davis to have a fresh point of view towards Indonesia, who have grown in the last 20 years to leave behind its authoritarian past and turning itself into a true democracy, with deep and abiding respect for human rights and playing the role of an active and constructive force for good in the region and beyond.

While thanking you for your kind attention, please accept, Sir, the assurances of our highest consideration.

Wiranto
Coordinating Minister for Political,
Judicial & Security Affairs

The letter was a strange departure for the usually tight-lipped former general, who has been accused of war crimes in East Timor. I'll never forget watching him be chased across a wet lawn in monsoonal rain in Dili in 1999 by the well-respected *Washington Post* correspondent Keith Richburg, a giant of a man, yelling, 'General, please can you tell us if you are funding the militia ... General, give me an answer.' The general ran back into the governor's residence, leaving Richburg still yelling questions in the rain. That, I thought at the time as a young journalist, was a real doorstop.

While the people fled, the OPM declared the province a war zone and stayed to fight. The reports dribbled out over the next few months – normally from the Indonesian side, from the state news agency Antara, or the English-language *Jakarta Post*, or sometimes the well-known *Tempo*. One Indonesian officer shot here, another three troops killed there, a six-hour firefight there. Six hours – that is a long one, I thought, reading the report. It reflected what I was seeing in photos sent to me from the conflict zone: well-armed Papuans. Fully equipped with body armour and camouflage and modern weapons. These were not the same forces I had encountered on the Papua New Guinea border or in Timika in 2003. Back then, they had a few worn-out AK-47s and M16s they had captured or bought from the Indonesians. The rest had a shabby collection of shotguns, spears and bows and arrows. It was almost sad when they lined up to parade and salute their flag in a jungle clearing on the PNG border. In Timika all they had were a few shotguns and a rusty old .38-calibre six-shooter that their leader, Goliath Tabuni, pointed directly at me as we conducted an interview in a so-called safe house on the outskirts of the town.

Back then, both leaders – Mathias Wenda on the northern border and Goliath Tabuni outside Timika – wanted one thing: guns. They wanted guns to fight the Indonesian military and police. To them, the choice was life in an Indonesian prison or succumbing to the domination of their land and their lives ... and that they would not accept. It was fight or die. They just needed the right weapons. And eventually, partly from Indonesian money siphoned off from the failed autonomy funding, they got them.

Now, as the Indonesian military responded to the killing of their road workers in the same old way – by sending in troops and helicopters, and threatening the local population with reprisals – they faced a very different OPM. Well armed, determined and disciplined. The local population fled but the fighters remained, and the Indonesians found their troops being ambushed, their officers shot by snipers and their patrols being pinned down in well-organised firefights by an enemy that did not back away as before.

*

Throughout 2019, the fighting in Nduga continued. More Indonesian troops out in the field, patrolling the thick jungles and the steep mountainous terrain, supported by helicopters and operating from small bases in the wilderness, meant more ambush targets for an energised, aggressive and now better-armed force of guerrillas acting in bands of no more than twenty. Their tactics were simple. They would lie in wait for the patrols they knew from their scouts were coming. They would choose an advantageous position and, when the moment was right, attack. Sometimes they would kill one or two, sometimes they would lose one of theirs. If the Indonesian force was overwhelming, they would scatter into the jungle. If it wasn't, they would stay and fight, sometimes chasing the patrol and recovering the weapons of the dead Indonesians. Often the Indonesians would ask for back-up and a helicopter or more troops would arrive. Then the Papuans would retreat further up to the mountains, knowing the Indonesians would not follow them. It is still going on like this now.

Ironically, the one way to glimpse a picture of this kind of war from the outside, as all journalists and foreigners are banned from the area, is through the Indonesian military statements, often published through the state news agency Antara. Updates, mostly concerning Indonesian casualties, are published regularly. One describes an exchange where an Indonesian soldier was killed and the patrol turned back, commenting that the terrain was too mountainous to recover his body. The OPM do put out their own statements, but due to the communications difficulties they are often much later, allowing the Indonesian military to give their version first.

Although sometimes the pattern is reversed: on 10 February 2020, the Indonesian military command announced they had found the remains of their helicopter that had gone missing on 28 June 2019, just minutes after take-off in Sentani. It had been heading toward the border with troops and supplies on board. Twelve people were killed in the crash. The local OPM commander announced he and his men had found the wreckage of the Russian-made Mi-17 helicopter on 5 February and took all the weapons and had long claimed they had shot it down. The wreckage couldn't be recovered, as it was on a ninety-degree cliffside. More than 1000 Indonesian troops who had been searching for the helicopter on the ground were despatched to the area.

In 2020 there have also been reports of the Indonesians triumphantly declaring the deaths of the 'separatist criminals' in Nduga and the discovery of arms caches, which they admitted had come from East Java. Occasionally the Papuans release reports of their own success in killing Indonesian soldiers in the field, flaunting the captured weapons in supplied photos. It is a brutal ongoing struggle being carried out in one of the most inhospitable and isolated parts of the world, and with no international access.

Twenty years ago this deceased man's father, the rebel leader Silas Kogoya, was filmed singing a song to his baby son – a lullaby telling him he should be careful or the Indonesians would kill him. When he came of age, they did, and they took photos.

West Papuan women and children prepare food in the jungle after fleeing Indonesian military operations in Nduga province in 2019.

DIPLOMACY

On 25 January 2019, Benny Wenda, exiled leader of the political arm of the West Papuan independence movement, handed a petition signed by 1.8 million West Papuans to the United Nations human rights chief Michelle Bachelet in Geneva. The actual hand-signed document, weighing more than 40 kilograms, had been collated and smuggled across the border to Papua New Guinea over a period of months in 2017. Representing more than 70 per cent of the West Papua and Papua provinces' population of 2.5 million, it requested the relisting of West Papua on the UN committee for decolonisation, from which it had been removed in 1963, and a UN-supervised independence vote.

Getting the document to the UN had resulted in the arrest and imprisonment of key Papuan activists. Yanto Awerkion, a local leader of the West Papua National Committee (Komite Nasional Papua Barat, or KNPB), was held in jail for eight months without trial for supporting the petition. More recently, the offices of the KNPB and the United Liberation Movement for West Papua (ULMWP) in West Papua were raided and key activists arrested. Five activists were arrested during a raid on

15 January 2019, reportedly because the authorities discovered their involvement in the petition. Three remain in prison on charges of treason.

But getting the document together under the noses of the Indonesian military and intelligence was only the start. Once the document had been transported out of the country there was another problem: actually getting it tabled. In September 2017, Benny Wenda tried to table it at the UN's decolonisation committee in New York. The chair of the committee, Rafael Ramírez, declined. 'I am the chair of the C24 and the issue of West Papua is not a matter for the C24,' he said. 'We are just working on the countries that are part of the list of non-self-governing territories. That list is issued by the general assembly.'[15]

He added that the decolonisation committee supported Indonesia's claim to the territory and that the issue of West Papua could not be on the agenda. As *The Guardian* reported, the Venezuelan diplomat was blunt in his rejection: 'The special committee on decolonisation has not received nor can receive any request or document related to the situation of West Papua,' he said, 'territory which is an integral part of the Republic of Indonesia.' *The Guardian* went on to note that Indonesia's representative to the UN, Dian Triansyah Djani, was a vice-chair of the decolonisation committee.[16]

It was a blow to the West Papuans, both inside and out, who had tried so hard under very difficult and dangerous conditions to compile this petition and say to the UN that after all these years they wanted their case revisited. The point was made over and over again that the UN-sponsored Act of Free Choice had been rigged, that the tiny proportion of the population who had been allowed to vote – less than 0.2 per cent, according to Wenda – had been intimidated. The Papuans had tried to get the issue back on the agenda, but they had been rebuffed. They had to find another way.

*

In May 2016, inside Papua, demonstrations in support of independence and a referendum had been met with mass arrests. Peaceful protests and civil disobedience had disastrous consequences in the regional centres of Sorong, Merauke, Wamena, Fak Fak and Manokwari. Arrests were made at similar rallies in Semarang in Java and Makassar in South Sulawesi. In all, 1888 people were arrested. As I wrote in *The Saturday Paper*:

> Photos and video circulating both on social media and local media show the masses of people arrested in Jayapura and taken to the Indonesian police compound – forced to sit in rows in the heat with their hands behind their backs and made to remove their clothes ... Activists were separated from the main group and put in cells at the main police headquarters. They were beaten – police stamping on their chests and backs and hitting them in the head with rifle butts ...
>
> Local journalists are under great threat and intimidation. At the time, media advocacy group Reporters

Sans Frontières (RSF) issued a statement condemning the arrest of a local journalist in the Jayapura protests and the prevention of other journalists covering the mass detention. The organisation quoted unnamed local journalists as saying police told them they were under orders to keep journalists away from the site. Police Commissioner Mathius Fakhiri was named as directly issuing the order to remove journalists, who were greeted by about 20 police wielding wooden batons to keep them away …

Earlier reports by RSF have documented and protested at the treatment of the few foreign journalists who have managed to get into Papua, as well as the harassment and intimidation of their local translators, drivers and fixers. If you ask Indonesian officials, they will say there is no press ban in Papua, you just have to go through the right process. But the complicated, lengthy and often futile series of permissions from anyone within Indonesian foreign affairs, or its police, military and intelligence services, means permission is rarely granted and strictly controlled. President Widodo promised to alleviate this but nothing has changed. Journalists are still getting arrested and deported. If they try to enter on a tourist visa, they are jailed. Local journalists are still harassed, monitored and jailed.

The Indonesian military are so concerned that Papua will be subject to international calls for independence they spy on everybody who takes an interest in Papuan events, politics and human rights. In 2011, leaked

> documents revealed that even though I hadn't been to or reported on Papua since 2003 I was on a list of 'Foreign Networks/Foreign Leaders in support of Free Papua' held by the Indonesian army special forces group, Kopassus. I came in at No. 9 on the list of Australians. Thirty-one other Australians were named, including then Greens leader Bob Brown at No. 13. The list identified current and former US senators. It also mentioned Bishop Desmond Tutu of South Africa and members of the British parliament, Lord Avebury and Jeremy Corbyn, who had both spoken publicly about West Papua. Also on the list were former PNG prime minister Sir Michael Somare, and former Vanuatu foreign minister Sir Barak Sope. In all, it lists 248 politicians, academics, environmentalists, journalists, artists and clergy, from Australia, Canada, New Zealand, Britain, the US, Germany, Finland, Ireland, the European Union, PNG and Vanuatu, calling them 'the supporters of Papuan separatists'.[17]

The reasons for the demonstrations in 2016 were both to mark the 1963 annexation of Dutch New Guinea (Papua) and to show support for a broad coalition of groups campaigning for independence, specifically the meeting of the International Parliamentarians for West Papua in London. The meeting, attended by ministers from Papua New Guinea and Vanuatu, the prime minister of Tonga, who was the group's co-founder, and British opposition leader Jeremy Corbyn, came out with an emphatic resolution: 'The UN must be allowed to organise a referendum to allow the people of West Papua to choose between acknowledging the incorporation of their country into Indonesia or voting for independence.' It was the high-profile recognition that had been demanded by the supporters of Papuan independence for years.

Australia made no comment on the declaration, and the Indonesian embassy in Canberra dismissed it as a 'publicity stunt'.[18] In fact, Australia remains silent on the arrests in Papua, the historical and current abuses by the Indonesian military there, and the calls for UN involvement and a resolution to the ongoing violence and isolation. Unlike in the late 1990s, when we finally intervened in East Timor and our conservative leaders took moral credit for its 'liberation' from Indonesian abuses, now our moral bank is empty. The Indonesians can always point to Manus Island and say they only arrested and beat pro-independence protesters for a day or so. Australia did it indefinitely just down the coast. Maybe that was why the story of the declaration didn't get much of a run.

*

Most of those arrested in 2016 were released, but their identities were noted, and the Indonesians tried systematically to identify, disrupt and compromise their networks. People were turned against one another with bribes or the simple tactic of offering them immunity from arrest if they cooperated with the Indonesian authorities, principally in identifying those involved in pro-independence activities. The Papuans, isolated and largely without contact with the outside world, sought ways to get their message out. Through social media, mobile phone video and limited, monitored phone calls they continued to try to impress upon the outside world the gravity of their situation.

In response, the Indonesians conducted their own social media campaigns. In 2019 the BBC reported on how apparently co-ordinated campaigns were seeking to skew international views of Papua. The investigation, by the BBC and the Australian Strategic Policy Institute (ASPI), identified a network of easily recognisable 'bots' – or automated accounts – which were sharing the same pro-government content about Papua at the same time. As the BBC reported:

> The Twitter accounts were all using fake or stolen profile photos, including images of K-pop stars or random people, and were clearly not functioning as 'real' people do on social media.
>
> This led to the discovery of a network of automated fake accounts spread across at least four social media platforms and numerous websites which could be traced to a Jakarta-based media company, InsightID.
>
> The bots would jump on to hashtags being used by groups supporting independence, such as #freewestpapua, so they swamped negative reporting with positive stories about investment in the region, a process known as 'hashtag hijacking'.
>
> This technique was also used on Facebook. One such message, in English, said Indonesia had invited the UN to

Papua to assess the situation. But the UN has complained that, despite an agreement more than a year ago, an official visit has still to take place.

The company pushed out content on Facebook with paid ads targeting users in the US, UK and Europe.

'The risk of a campaign like this, in a place with so little access to truly independent media, is it skews the perceptions and understanding of the international community in a way that doesn't reflect reality,' says ASPI cyber researcher Elise Thomas.

'That appears to be the goal, one which someone is willing to spend hundreds of dollars and many months to achieve.'[19]

In January 2020, Reuters revealed how the Indonesian military facilitated this. 'As Indonesia celebrated its National Heroes' Day last year,' the article began, 'official military social media accounts lavished praise on Corporal Yunanto Nugroho for the "myriad awards he has won in the field of IT".' The piece went on to outline why:

> Yunanto co-ordinates a network of websites facilitated and funded by the military that publishes pro-government propaganda under the guise of independent news, according to web registration records and Reuters interviews with website editors and a special forces intelligence officer.
>
> The sites publish content that supports the conduct of the military and police in quashing a separatist uprising

> in the Indonesian provinces in Papua, a fight that has long been led by the country's elite special forces, Kopassus.
>
> Colonel Muhammad Aidi, an intelligence adviser to a Kopassus commander who bestowed an award on Yunanto in November, told Reuters the army computer operator had helped create and sustain many news websites as part of 'military efforts' in partnership with civilian volunteers that included youths and media veterans who had approached the military to help.

Reuters tracked the domain names of several 'news' websites to a military base in Jakarta. The ten websites, the article said,

> do not disclose their links to the military, and in recent months most of them have made their domain information private. The websites publish uniformly positive coverage of government, military and police alongside articles that demonize government critics and human rights investigators. The subjects of some stories told Reuters the websites attributed invented quotes to them and published other falsehoods.[20]

The article also noted the websites were given 'thank you payments' from the Indonesian military for their work.

The disinformation campaign enables the Indonesian government and military to present a counter-narrative acceptable to countries that support them, trade with them, and train and supply their military. In short, it lets those countries off the hook and allows them to do nothing about the ongoing human rights abuses in West Papua.

Today, the Trans-Papua Highway is being promoted online as a grand achievement. Well-produced YouTube videos show the project as a great adventure, with guys on off-road motorbikes making the muddy journey over half-built sections of the highway. To a soundtrack of heavy metal and dance music, and with lots of thrills and spills, they depict the road as the ultimate challenge, in the vein of *Top Gear* or a reality TV show.

*

Benny Wenda and his international supporters continued to try to find a way to present the petition to the UN. The chance finally came on 25 January 2019. With the help of the delegation from Vanuatu, Wenda was included in their group, which was scheduled to meet Michelle Bachelet in Geneva. He was able to present the 40-kilogram document to Bachelet, who said she had no previous knowledge of its existence. Her response was positive. She was pictured with Wenda, smilingly receiving the massive tome containing the original signatures demanding the UN put the issue of West Papua back on the decolonisation list in order to eventually oversee a referendum and to appoint a delegate to West Papua to investigate human rights abuses.

Her spokeswoman, Ravina Shamdasani, said that Bachelet had informed the Vanuatu delegation that the UN Human Rights Office 'has been engaging with the Indonesian authorities on the issue of Papua, including the prevailing human rights situation, and has requested access to Papua'.[21]

To Wenda and the United Liberation Movement for West Papua, the result was historic and a major step forward. In a statement issued after the handover, Wenda said:

> The people of West Papua have been crying out for support for over 50 years. The time for the UN to hear this call is more urgent than ever as the world witnesses another humanitarian crisis happening in the highlands of West Papua ...
>
> Today, thousands of civilians in the region of Nduga are fleeing from the Indonesian military, escaping airstrikes and chemical weapons. Whilst children die from starvation, the Indonesian military block all aid or investigation ...
>
> And to the people of West Papua, thank you. Today is a proud moment to represent your voices – thank you for never giving up and for courageously coming to the streets and flying the Morning Star flag, despite the brutality you face ... Thank you for your patience, your strength and your spirit. Thank you to so many of you for having the courage to sign the historic People's Petition – your voice is now in the hands of the UN. We are making progress, together, in unity.[22]

The Indonesian response was not quite so generous. Indonesia's delegate to the UN said Vanuatu had 'deliberately deceived' Bachelet, according to Associated Press. Indonesia 'would never retreat to defend and protect' its territorial sovereignty. After this, the UN repeated its request to send a delegation to West Papua and initially the Indonesian president agreed. But the visit still has not gone ahead. A request by NZ diplomats to send representatives, particularly to Nduga, in 2019 was rebuffed, and no other diplomats have been allowed to visit the area. Australia did not even protest the ban and did not request to visit the province.

*

Meanwhile, in the highlands town of Wamena, an example was being made by the Indonesian authorities. In August 2018, Polish tourist Jakub Fabian Skrzypski became the first foreigner to be arrested for treason in Indonesia. Simon Magal, a pro-independence activist with whom Skrzypski communicated, was also arrested the following month. Initially the charge included intending to sell weapons and ammunition to the local OPM. The authorities were trying to build a case for a twenty-year sentence, claiming he had met with local pro-independence Papuans in the highland town for this purpose. In fact, Skryzpski was just a tourist, and in the highlands of West Papua, speaking to a pro-independence Papuan is almost unavoidable.

As he languished in jail in Wamena in January 2019, he spoke to US-funded Asian news agency BenarNews, who managed to get in to see him. Skrzypski denied being involved in arms smuggling or propaganda on behalf of Papuan rebels:

> 'I am not a blogger or filmmaker, journalist or activist. I am not a military trainer and I do not have that background. I am not an arms dealer,' Skrzypski told BenarNews on Jan. 9 …
>
> During interrogation, police kept showing a photo of him in Switzerland and one of him shaking hands with someone as evidence, he said.
>
> 'What do those photos prove? Are they trying to trap me for some political reason, their own ambition, or personal gain?'[23]

He later complained that the Indonesian authorities had prevented Polish consular assistance being given to him and that his incarceration was the result of an irrational fear of foreigners in the region and had occurred for propaganda and political purposes.

Eventually Jakob and his friend Simon, whom he had met on Facebook, went to trial in Wamena, and were convicted of treason on 2 May 2019, with the Pole receiving five years and his friend four years. Skrzypski told Associated Press it was unjust that his trial had taken place in this remote location, making it difficult for his lawyers to represent him adequately.

He compared his case to that of two French journalists who were arrested in Wamena in 2014 after entering the region on tourist visas to report on independence fighters. Their trial took place in the capital, Jayapura, and they were sentenced to ten weeks in prison. Speaking to the BBC after the conviction, Skrzypski said he had not had a chance to state his case at the trial, whereas Papua police spokesperson Suryadi Diaz said that they had evidence he was involved in arms trading. 'He was involved in buying ammunition for them,' Diaz told BBC Indonesia, but Skrzypski strongly denied those accusations: 'My trip wasn't a clandestine one. I was visiting friends. This conflict is irrelevant to me. I don't even know it very well.'[24] Skrzypski said his Indonesian friends were afraid to show their support: 'They don't dare to voice it, to speak up. They are afraid of troubles that they think the police and prosecutors may cause them. Same applies to my potential witnesses.'[25]

It was one of the worst examples in a long list of expulsions, arrests and interrogations of any foreigner visiting the provinces.

*

Following the tabling of the petition, the various groups from outside and inside West Papua working towards a referendum and eventual independence met in the capital of Papua New Guinea. They held a rare press conference on 31 January 2019. The event was significant in that it was the first time all the different groups had met and agreed on a joint communique. The message was simple: they supported the continued fighting in the highlands, they supported continued civil protests in the towns and villages against the Indonesians, and they supported and called for the involvement of the UN to oversee a referendum for West Papua. Although Wenda admitted they had no control over those fighting in the highlands, his acknowledgement and approval of their struggle symbolised a shift in the mood of the Papuan groups who had long advocated for peaceful change. It was in effect a declaration of war.

The message resonated with some PNG leaders, tired of dealing with a seemingly endless West Papuan refugee problem on their border. A few prominent politicians, including the governor of Port Moresby, weighed in, saying the UN had a responsibility to help them deal with the latest influx of Papuans fleeing the fighting in Nduga. The communique also met with some support from PNG MPs, a few of whom mentioned they would pursue it in parliament.

The diplomatic struggle continued in August 2019, when a Papuan delegation attended the Pacific Islands Forum held in Tuvalu. According to the ABC's *Pacific Beat*,

> Leaders of the Pacific Islands Forum have urged Indonesia to take action over their concerns at ongoing human rights violations in West Papua.
>
> The final communique of the Forum, held in Tuvalu last week, also called on Jakarta to finalise the timing of a visit by the UN High Commissioner for Human Rights to allow for a report to be prepared ahead of next year's leaders meeting.
>
> Ronny Kareni, Pacific representative of the United Liberation Movement for West Papua, ULMWP, welcomed the language used in the communique.
>
> 'In terms of the language … it's a strong push by the leaders,' he said.

'In particular, calling on the UN Commissioner for Human Rights, that's a big step.'[26]

But the Indonesians, of course, voiced their objections to the very presence of West Papuans at the forum. A spokesman told *The Guardian* that 'Jakarta was "not at all happy" West Papua had been included on the formal agenda for the forum leaders' meeting in Tuvalu, and warned the move would establish a precedent for interference in other countries' domestic affairs.'[27]

Slowly, slowly, with the help of a few Melanesian island nations, the West Papuan cause and the push for a referendum was getting back on the international agenda. But while this happened, another round of violence was beginning.

THE STUDENTS

It was a simple insult that started it. *Monkey*. The Indonesian police alongside Islamic and nationalist Indonesians gathered outside the Papuan university dormitory in the East Javanese city of Surabaya and yelled 'Monkey' at the Papuan students inside. One story said the Papuans had flushed the Indonesian flag down the toilet. Another said they threw it in a drain. Another said they pulled it down and replaced it with the Morning Star. Whatever happened to start the trouble, the result was a huge crowd of angry Indonesians and police screaming at the Papuans to get out and go back to Papua. The chant was 'Monkeys go home', pretty much, in various translations.

It was 17 August 2019, Indonesia's day to celebrate the declaration of Independence from the Dutch in 1945. It had been a national holiday since the 1950s, when President Sukarno declared it one. For these Indonesians, it was too much of an insult that Papuans could tear down their flag on such a day. One of Sukarno's greatest achievements was saving the 'monkeys' from colonialism under the Dutch – how dare these ingrates desecrate the flag? Word spread, a crowd formed. The

Papuans stayed inside and pretty soon the police turned up.

The Papuans inside were remarkably defiant, with one apparently telling a reporter, 'If I cannot fly my flag, they cannot fly theirs.' Having seen Papuan students demonstrating at the university in Abepura and security forces there trying to round them up, I can well believe it. They were like rugby players, taking people down right and left.

The difference was this time Papuans, and those sympathetic to them, were filming it all on their phones. They put it on Twitter, Facebook and every other social media platform they could find. Here was an incident of racism and abuse clearly documented and clearly sanctioned in by the Indonesian state. They were second-class citizens in their own country. The best and brightest had been sent off to university in Surabaya and still they were called monkeys and dogs. It filtered back to West Papua pretty quickly, and widespread rioting and demonstrations commenced two days later.

On 19 August the massive protests, involving thousands of people, started in Jayapura and the towns of Manokwari, Sorong and Wamena. They quickly escalated to violence, with government buildings burnt down and even the airport briefly seized by protesters in Sorong. The scale of the protest and the determination of the protesters not to back down in the face of the usual security services response were unprecedented. Thousands took to the streets. They were chanting calls for independence, waving the Morning Star flag, condemning the institutional racism in Indonesian society that had labelled their students in Surabaya monkeys.

But there was more, so much more, behind the protests. The entire sentiment of disenfranchisement, of marginalisation, oppression and brutalisation by Indonesian society, suffused the protesters. More than fifty years of it. It was like a dam of emotion and frustration had been breached and the Papuans flowed out onto the streets, an unstoppable flood. The Indonesian human rights lawyer Veronica Koman told France 24, 'I've never seen the Papuans so angry.'[28] There are no figures on how many people took part, but Koman said that it was the first time Papuan protests had reached this magnitude.

The anger continued the following week. The prison in Sorong was partially burnt down, allowing more than 250 prisoners to escape. Government buildings in Manokwari, Sorong, Fak Fak and Wamena were also burnt down by protesters, sometimes with people inside. The Indonesian military and police opened fire with live ammunition on the demonstrators, but this time it only seemed to anger them more. They refused to back down, and extended their protests to Indonesian shops and businesses, burning them down.

The Indonesians flew in more troops. They shut down the internet in West Papua, as well as all mobile phone coverage, landline phones and even ATM access. They were losing control, and they did not want anyone in the outside world to see it.

Meanwhile, people were dying. The worst was in Wamena, where it was reported in *The New Zealand Herald* by long-time campaigner for East Timor and West Papua Maire Leadbeater that, on 23 September:

> Forty-three people were killed as buildings and vehicles were torched. More than half of the victims were non-Papuan migrants and many residents, both Papuan and non-Papuan, fled the area. Jakarta capitalised on the suffering of the migrants, offering them trauma counselling and flights home. Journalists were banned and the internet closed off, but some recent witness accounts suggest provocateurs may have been involved.[29]

Lurid and graphic tales of the fate of Indonesian 'settlers' were run in the press, highlighting the trauma and threats the Indonesian transmigrants had experienced. Indonesian military C-130 aircraft were flown in to evacuate them and the Papuans were portrayed once again as savages and out of control. What the papers didn't report was how many Papuans were being shot, arrested and tortured by the security forces, who were trying to repel this huge tide of anger and resentment. The Surabaya 'monkey' video had been, as one commentator put it, 'the straw that broke the camel's back'. The fighting in the highlands, the diplomatic efforts abroad and the continuing economic marginalisation of the Papuans signified by such mega-projects as the Trans-Papua Highway had created a pressure-cooker environment that exploded with the demonstrations, which on more than one occasion descended into full-blown riots.

With the internet and communications blackout, the narrative of the Indonesians as victims crept into international coverage. But the reality was the Indonesian security personnel were cracking down as hard as they could in the usual way.

As renowned Indonesian novelist Eka Kurniawan put it in *The New York Times*,

> The crackdown targets not just Papuans, but anyone who sympathizes with their struggle. Surya Anta Ginting, the spokesman for the Indonesian People's Front for West Papua, was arrested alongside the students, also on treason charges. While in detention, he reportedly was held in isolation and made to listen to nationalist songs.
>
> Veronica Koman, a lawyer for the West Papua National Committee, a pro-independence group, has been accused of provoking the violence by spreading fake news, simply because she shared information about Papua on Twitter. She is thought to be in Australia, and the Indonesian police have asked Interpol to arrest her and have threatened to revoke her passport.
>
> Once again, a crisis in Papua is revealing the true face of the Indonesian government. This is an Indonesian government that, rather than listen to the Papuan people's cries for dignity and equity, tries to quiet them with soldiers and money. This is an Indonesian government that allows Papuan people to be called monkeys and then asks them simply to forgive.[30]

Into September, Papuan civil society raged in protest in the information vacuum that the Indonesian government had created. Foreigners were barred and any who were there were thrown out. Four Australians were arrested and deported after being near a protest in Sorong. The violence continued, with 6000 more troops and police deployed to West Papua.

A student dormitory in Abepura, just outside the capital Jayapura, was attacked by security forces and local pro-Indonesian militia, who opened fire on the students inside, killing three. That incident was caught on video. It seemed nothing could stop the killing. The Indonesian security forces had their blood boiling, but so did the Papuans. The Indonesians complained that their police had been attacked in their cars by angry students throwing rocks and arrows in the Abepura incident. The fact they had just shot dead three students was downplayed.

Footage emerged showing soldiers firing at a crowd of demonstrators outside a government office in Deiyai. Some of the demonstrators were standing with their hands in the air as soldiers moved in. It was always a few here, a few there. Papuans were killed and arrested; Indonesian transmigrants were killed, or their businesses and government buildings burnt down, in revenge. The reports of violence continued to come in from Jayapura, Sorong, Manokwari, Timika, Fak Fak and Wamena – all the major population centres. A theme started to emerge: the presence of pro-Indonesian militias composed of Indonesian loyalists from the migrant population or from Islamic organisations that were clearly supported by – and in some cases, such as the Abepura student dormitory attack, integrated with – the police.

I wasn't surprised by those reports. Ever since I first went to West Papua in 2002, the Papuans had been talking about the threats they received from groups such as Laskar Jihad, who viewed themselves as defenders of Indonesia and Indonesians in West Papua. The pattern was a nationalist group moving in and starting trouble, tolerated, indeed encouraged, by the local Indonesian police and military. It was fine for them to walk around on the streets yelling Islamic and nationalistic slogans and carrying swords and knives. But if you did that as a Papuan, you would be shot on the spot.

*

When I read the report of the attack on the student dormitory in Abepura and the involvement of Islamic nationalist militias, I couldn't help but think about the last phone call I received from the Australian filmmaker Mark Worth, in 2004. He was in Sentani, near Abepura. He had just completed a landmark film for the ABC called *Land of the Morning Star*, which is still the most accurate telling of the West Papuan story to date. He had largely dedicated his life to telling this story. Growing up on Manus Island in Papua New Guinea, then administered by Australia, he was no stranger to the region. Before the film was aired, he returned to West Papua. When he left Melbourne, I had given him a copy of Ryszard Kapuściński's book *Another Day of Life* to read on the plane. He called me on my mobile some time afterward. 'It is just like the book here – there are militias everywhere, I am getting followed. Seriously, it has got far worse than when you were here last year. It is fucking intense,' he yelled into the phone as I strained to hear him over the Melbourne traffic.

Unbeknown to Mark, the ABC international channel broadcast his documentary while he was in Jayapura. He had gone to West Papua to see his estranged West Papuan wife and young daughter before the film was to be broadcast, because he knew that after it aired he would be targeted. And that is exactly what happened. When he called me, he was in Sentani, near the airport. He was trying to get a flight out. He was being followed and threatened by the Indonesian security forces. He was under extreme pressure and thought every day would be his last.

That was the last time I ever heard from him. He died in his hotel room, either on the night of 15 January 2004 or the next day. The Indonesian authorities buried him before an autopsy could be carried out, and refused to exhume his body when his long-time friend, the investigative journalist Mark Davis, flew up there later to try to find out what had happened.

Many people may disagree with me. Mark Worth was not in good health when he went to Indonesia. But from the tone of that phone call – what he said, the sound of his voice and how he described the way the Indonesians operated with their militias – I remain convinced the Indonesian authorities or those aligned with them, such as the militias, killed him.

We had talked at length about the risks of him returning. He was well known to the Indonesian authorities. He had been heavily critical of them in the past. He had just made a landmark film telling the story of the West Papuans, going back to their first contact with the outside world and the brutal introduction they received into the twentieth century at the hands and the guns of the Indonesians. I remember trying to talk him out of going, saying, 'Mate, they will just kill you.' But he went anyway. I knew after that phone call he was in serious trouble. Next thing I heard he was dead.

I wrote an obituary for him. I was crying as I did it. He truly was a man who put himself up against an immovable force that was, and still is, an Indonesian occupation, and like so many unnamed Papuans, he was killed. Finally, after he was dead, the ABC ran his film in Australia, with barely any promotion or publicity. The internal politics of the ABC and their concerns over the content and its coverage of the independence movement, which Mark had railed against as he was putting the finishing touches on the film in Melbourne, seemed to have played out to a tragic conclusion. It was narrated by Cate Blanchett. I am not sure if he would have liked the final edit. But he was not around to see it. He was in the ground in West Papua.

*

The stories that do get out of Papua are only the tip of the iceberg. Take this incident from September 2019, reported in *The Guardian*:

> Indonesian police are investigating allegations of masked motorcycle riders throwing bags of snakes into a West Papuan student dormitory in Surabaya and 'deliberately spreading terror'.
>
> The hostel was the site of anti-Papua protests last month, which then sparked rolling and often violent

protests across Indonesia, including in the Papuan province.

Students at the East Java accommodation, which was the target of racist taunts and protests last month, said shortly after 4am Monday four people on two motorcycles pulled up outside the building.

They threw an open sack containing a 15–20kg python, and another containing three 'aggressive' snakes which escaped into the compound, student Yohanes Giyai told the *Guardian*.[31]

The students managed to catch all but one of the snakes. But the incident reflected the perpetrators' sense of impunity when it came to the Indonesian security forces – if indeed they were not part of the security forces themselves.

But it doesn't all go one way. On 30 December 2019, the *Jakarta Globe* reported an attack on an Indonesian patrol in the border region of Papua and Papua New Guinea:

The body of Sergeant Miftakfur will be flown to Semarang, Central Java, before being buried in his hometown in Demak.

Papua Police Chief Insp. Gen. Paulus Waterpau said an OPM group led by Jefri Pagawak and Jemi Wenda was responsible for the attack. Jemi is a son of Matias Wenda, an OPM leader currently based in Bewani in Papua New Guinea.

'The two men and four other OPM members

used three guns to attack the soldiers, killing one of them,' Paulus said on Monday.

A team made up of Indonesian Military (TNI) and National Police officers has been despatched to catch the attackers.[32]

It was another case of the sons of the old leaders taking up the fight against the Indonesians from their remote camps. As I found in both East Timor and Aceh, there is generally a twenty-year cycle in the violence. One generation is killed, jailed and suppressed, and the next generation starts the fight again.

*

The students are part of a wave of empowerment of younger Papuans, who know their rights and are ready to stand up for and die for them, just as their fathers and mothers have before them. This is a female as well as a male story. The long history of sexual abuse of Papuan women detained or involved in military operations in Papua is well documented, but in a case in late 2019, one Papuan woman spoke out.

As reported in *The Jakarta Post* on 5 December 2019:

The allegations came to light after the prisoner told her lawyer that she had been sexually harassed by two policemen, identified only by the initials RO and W.

'The sexual abuse occurred twice. Once on the morning of Nov. 14 and then on Dec. 2,' the woman's lawyer

> Yohanis Mambrasar said.
>
> Yohanis said that the first incident occurred in the Papua Police's visitation room at around 10:00 a.m. on Nov. 14, when the prisoner was sweeping the room. RO entered the room and asked her to have sex with him.
>
> 'According to the victim, RO asked her to have sex four times, but she ignored him,' Yohanis said, adding that the incident scared her and left her unable to sleep.
>
> The prisoner reported the incident to a female police officer named Welly, who told her to tell any other officers who tried to harass her that she would report them to Welly.
>
> Yohanis said the second incident occurred when another officer, W, came to her cell during the early hours of Dec. 2.
>
> The prisoner awoke when she felt someone sitting on her bed. Once she was awake, W started asking her questions, starting from questions about her family to more personal questions, ending with W asking her to have sex with him.[33]

According to the report, the woman screamed to alert other prisoners. It worked. The fact the incidents happened is no surprise, but the fact the prisoner spoke out about it is new. The younger, educated, articulate and politically aware Papuans will continue to force the issues of fair treatment under Indonesian law and a review of the Act of Free Choice that put them under that law. They all know the history; they have all grown up with the repression. They have grown up fighting, whether it has been in the demonstrations in the towns, with their subsequent shootings and arrests by the security forces, or in the bush and the villages, with the military sweeps and air attacks. Even abroad, in the camps of PNG. They have seen their leaders shot and jailed. They live with the Indonesian military post on the corner. The searches, the document checks, the beatings, the arrests, the surveillance and the swaggering, casual violence of the Indonesian military and police who come and go on what they consider to be their 'tour of duty' in a war zone. They all have one thing in common: an overwhelming desire to right a historic wrong.

I've seen it on the faces of people on a bus when it is stopped by the military. In a market when a patrol comes through. In the reaction of students protesting when the police and military inevitably show up to make arrests and beat people and sometimes shoot them. They are defiant, but they are also afraid. They know the stories of torture, beatings and arbitrary arrest, as well as deaths at the hands of the security forces. It is their own fathers, mothers, uncles, aunts and grandparents who have gone through this. They have lived with the presence of those permanently damaged by the Indonesian authorities and their own violent oppression. They are remarkably kind and understanding to those among them who can no longer work or look after themselves because they have emerged alive but permanently damaged, physically and mentally, from the Indonesian system.

*

It is not only young Papuans with skin in this fight. It is common to encounter younger Indonesians who are appalled by their own government and the actions of its security services. The brave and outspoken students who drove the Suharto government from power in 1998 and made way for a more open and democratic society do not buy the resurgent nationalism and cronyism of the military and political elite. They were there in 1998 and '99 in East Timor, and in Aceh from 2000 to 2003. One of the most prominent was Munir, whom I met in both places many times in those years. He was a fearless promoter and documenter of the human rights abuses of the Indonesian state. He was killed by a cup of poisoned orange juice on a Garuda flight to the Netherlands in 2004.

Another prominent young Indonesian fighting for justice for West Papua is human rights lawyer Veronica Koman. The Indonesian security services went after her for disseminating false news, because she had tweeted about the deteriorating situation in Papua in August, September and into October 2019. She was charged in absentia. They asked Interpol to issue a red notice to have her deported from Australia, where she had fled following an overwhelming online campaign to discredit her work and attack and threaten her and her family.

She was interviewed by Reuters in Sydney in October 2019:

> Veronica Koman, a human rights lawyer sought by Indonesian police over Twitter posts authorities blame

> for fanning unrest in the Papua region, has a tattoo on each wrist.
>
> The first, inked when she was in her late teens and a fervent nationalist, reads simply 'Indonesia' and, she says, meant that 'Indonesia is running through my veins'.
>
> The second, which she got a few years later after becoming 'exposed to social justice', has become a defiant riposte to the vitriol she has received for defending activists and advocating self-determination for Papua, Indonesia's easternmost provinces.
>
> The tattoo reads 'DILLIGAF', an abbreviation for a crude saying which roughly stands for 'Do I look like I give a damn?'

Reuters, following editorial guidelines, was too polite to say what the 'F' actually stood for.

'I've actually been experiencing this weird systematic attack, if you like, online since I think it was almost two years ago,' Koman told Reuters.

> The threats can come in slickly produced video posted on YouTube or comments from anonymous social media accounts.
>
> The abuse includes death threats, incitements to sexual assault and racist slurs, online material reviewed by Reuters showed. It also includes the publication of personal information about her and her family.
>
> 'I have never, ever published anything personal about

me on social media. Not even fun photos with friends. It's precisely because I knew that my work is very risky,' she said.

'It was information that's only available on family (identification) cards ... I have a feeling it was state-backed, otherwise who else?'[34]

Koman was charged by Indonesia in September 2019. The following month she received the prestigious Australian Sir Ronald Wilson Human Rights Award for her work on behalf of West Papuans. She dedicated the award to those Papuans she had relied on to help her compile the evidence to challenge the Indonesian government and military. 'Especially the dozens who have died at the hands of security forces, and the twenty-two political prisoners charged with treason over the past couple of months,' she told Radio New Zealand.

'I have the West Papuan people to thank for changing my life. They have taught me how to be resilient, how to keep fighting, how to keep going in circumstances where many outsiders may feel they have to stop.'

Marc Purcell, the chief executive of the Australian Council for International Development, which awards the prize, said the award represented 'the strength and bravery of all people who defend the human rights of West Papuans, who will not be silenced, and who will work towards a world where the human rights of all are protected and upheld'.

> 'Veronica has shone a light on violations of the rights of the West Papuan people at great personal cost,' he said.
>
> He also called on Australia to protect Koman and urge Indonesia to drop the charges against her.[35]

The Australian government has repeatedly indicated it does not care. When I was in West Papua in 2002 and 2003 I shared a laugh with a diplomat I met over dinner at a high-end hotel. I asked him about the Australian diplomats, whether they ever came to Papua. He replied with the old phrase: *Hear no evil, see no evil.* We both laughed cynically at that underlying truth. To his knowledge, they never went there and did not want to know what was going on. Then they could never be called to account.

West Papuan men build a temporary refuge in the jungle as they escape Indonesian troops in the highlands in 2019. They also use these dwellings to escape Indonesian military attacks from the air. Temperatures in the mountains often drop to single figures despite the equatorial location.

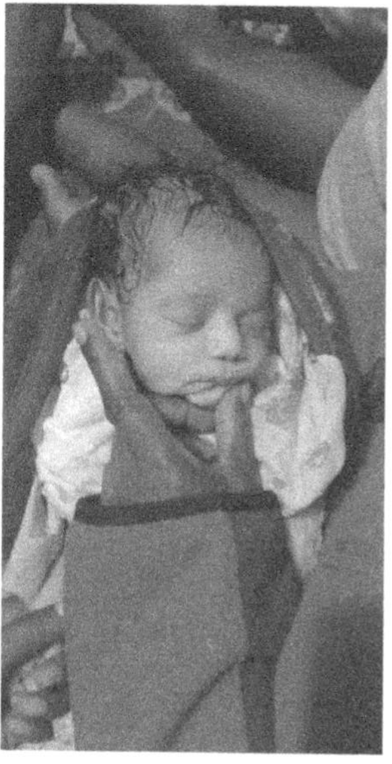

On 2 February 2020, Putri Santika Kamarigi, a baby aged one week and one day, died in a refugee camp after fleeing Indonesian military action in Nduga.

THE ANNIVERSARY

On 1 December 2019, one year after the killings of Indonesian roadworkers by the OPM, a military chopper was descending into a remote Indonesian military post in Nduga. Volleys of gunfire erupted from the surrounding jungle. On the ground, the Indonesian troops rushed to their firing positions. The gunfire was so intense from the surrounding bush that the helicopter, full of troops and supplies, flew away, back to base. A two-hour gunfight ensued between the Papuans and the Indonesians. This time the Papuans did not melt into the jungle. They stayed and fought. Only one Papuan casualty was reported by Indonesian news agency Antara. But the fact the Papuans had tried to ambush the resupply chopper and forced it to leave without landing spoke volumes about the new reality faced by Indonesian troops in this region. The time it took them to fight the Papuans off also said a lot about the new weaponry and adequate supplies the independence fighters had. In the past it would have been a few shots and then they would flee back into the jungle. Now it was a set-piece ambush initiated by the Nduga OPM.

Fifty-eight years since the first flag-raising in what was

then the Dutch-controlled capital known as Hollandia, now Jayapura, the Indonesians still could not control the highlands. They had tried bombing, garrisons, even chemical weapons; moving in Indonesian settlers, palm oil plantations, foreign logging and mining companies. They were still trying to pacify this area. They couldn't even resupply their own troops. Work on the great Trans-Papua Highway was moving ahead slowly, with sections being laid from Wamena, but now the work was being carried out by the military, as the threats to civilian workers had become too great.

The preparations for the anniversary of the flag-raising on 1 December had been going on for weeks. More Indonesian troops were flown into Jayapura, Wamena and Timika, including the special forces, Kostrad. In a series of bizarre displays of Indonesian military force, fully armed paratroopers were dropped in broad daylight over Wamena, Timika and Jayapura. In Timika they just dropped them over the airfield; the soldiers, wearing Santa hats but in full military gear, promptly handed out sweets to the local children who had come out to watch. It was a strange show of force and benevolence to instil both fear and appreciation in the local population. In reality it achieved neither.

As the anniversary approached, the police were busy. They stationed extra patrols and posts in all the major population centres. They carried out raids and arrested pro-independence suspects. People were detained for the slightest reasons. One Papuan was arrested following a midnight raid on his house in Wamena for having a kitchen knife in his pocket. This has to be set against the fact that local Indonesian militias were joining police in opposing demonstrations carrying swords, knives and in some cases guns.

The police commanders in West Papua called for peace and calm, while simultaneously conducting operations to intimidate and jail anyone they suspected of organising some kind of demonstration or flag-raising ceremony. It was a classic counter-insurgency operation from the Vietnam War era. Be nice to the townsfolk, promise money, peace and development. Show your military supremacy with displays of might, but at the same time demonstrate your kindness. Give sweets to the kids, hand out a bit of food here or there. Build them a road.

Reading the reports and analysing what was coming out from Papua in the weeks before 1 December 2019, I recalled the words of an American sergeant major briefing his troops as they were about to go on patrol in the Iraqi province of Diyala, at the height of the surge in 2007. 'You either kill 'em or treat them with dignity and respect.' At the time I thought, Hang on, that isn't going to work. The Indonesians were trying hard to do the same thing in Papua in 2018 and 2019. It didn't work out well for the Americans – Diyala became a hotbed of Islamic State activity when they pulled out. And it isn't working in Papua for the Indonesians. This is how the 1 December anniversary and preceding days unfolded, according to BenarNews:

> At least thirty-eight people in Indonesia's easternmost provinces were named treason suspects over the last

week in connection with attempts to raise the Papuan flag, police and lawyers told BenarNews.

Dozens more were arrested and questioned as security forces moved to prevent flag-raisings on Dec. 1, which some Papuans consider their national day …

Twenty people arrested Saturday in Sentani, an area near the Papuan provincial capital of Jayapura, are expected to be charged with treason, Yohanis Mambrasar, a lawyer with the Papua Human Rights Advocates Association (PAHAM), confirmed to BenarNews … Of these, six also will be charged with possessing weapons and one will face charges of incitement, said Victor Makbon, the police chief in Jayapura …

Seven people arrested in Manokwari, a coastal town in West Papua province, were being held for questioning after being picked up on Nov. 27, a local police official said.

'They are still under police custody at Manokwari Police Headquarters, while investigators are still looking for a man with the initials A.N.' who allegedly incited them to hold a protest, said Musa J. Permana, who heads the Crime and Research Unit at the regency's police department …

Meanwhile, West Papua Police Chief Brig. Gen. Herry Rudolf Nahak said police had arrested 11 people and charged them with treason after a flag-raising ceremony on Dec. 1 at Puncak Malanu, in Sorong, another coastal town in West Papua province.

> Arrests also took place in Fakfak, on the southern coast of West Papua, including dozens who allegedly attempted to raise a flag at the official residence of the regent, the top local official. Twenty of these people allegedly had cards stating they were members of the West Papuan National Liberation Army (TPNPB) ...
>
> 'About 20 will be named treason suspects,' he said.
>
> Two leaders of the United Liberation for West Papua were questioned by police in Jayapura over an appeal to worship to commemorate Dec. 1.
>
> Four men arrested during worship at Gembala Baik Church in the largely Christian province were released without charges early Monday after questioning, according to LBH Papua, the Papua Branch of Indonesian Legal Aid Foundation. The pastor of the church, James Kossay, was also questioned by police and released.[36]

The butcher's bill for Papua on 1 December 2019 was relatively light, thankfully. But only because the Indonesians had conducted extensive police and military operations beforehand. They had arrested leaders, killed Papuans, burnt down villages, broken up demonstrations with live gunfire and, with support from their local militia, killed and jailed students and demonstrators. In all, roughly a hundred people were arrested. Many faced treason charges, which carry a prison sentence of anywhere from five to twenty years. It was a pre-emptive move, mostly to deny the people the opportunity to attend flag-raisings in even the most remote places. The Indonesians had also conducted an extensive internet campaign to present the conflict in a different light, to the point that Twitter and YouTube had started shutting down the Indonesian-based accounts. There were demonstrations and arrests in other population centres, but mostly people stayed at home. By now the Papuans were playing the long game – diplomatically, in civil society, and militarily, in the bush – with a clear goal: a referendum for West Papua.

In 2003, even in the most remote places I could get to, speaking to those who had never had a day of school, who could neither read nor write, I found they would still quote you the entire history of the Indonesian takeover. From the first landings to the UN New York agreement to the Act of Free Choice in 1969 – they knew it all. Dates, events, attacks and the scale of the casualties at the hands of the Indonesian forces were seared into their minds by their own experience or the recollections of their elders. Then another generation came through. Educated, articulate, brave and defiant. It is they who have carried the struggle against the Indonesians to the higher, multi-layered level that we see today.

Civilians fleeing through the mountains. No foreign aid or observers are allowed into the province and these people live off food they collect or carry with them. At least 238 have been confirmed dead by church sources in 2019 but many, many more are unaccounted for due to their isolation and suspicion of outsiders.

EPILOGUE

There is the other side of the coin as well. I remember docking in the harbour at Jayapura on a large Pelni ship. It was full of Indonesian soldiers and nervous transmigrants from other parts of Indonesia, mostly Java. I had been on the boat for three days, coming from Kupang in West Timor, but most of the passengers were from Java and had been onboard for a week. It was an old ship that had been plying this route since the late 1970s. Faded murals showing happy Indonesians sowing and harvesting fields in this bounteous new land lined the walls in the dining room. Down in third class, amid the overflowing toilets and the piles of luggage, screaming babies and masses of people splayed out on the hard wooden benches that passed as beds and living quarters for those moving to West Papua, I spoke to the passengers about what they expected there. They were poor, mainly rural people – they had been offered land in West Papua and had decided to take it. Their expectations were modest. Some talked of farming the land; others spoke of opening a shop of some kind. When I asked them if they were worried about living in a new land, they dismissed it. Papua is Indonesia, they said, why should we worry?

Upstairs, in the second- and first-class areas, the military sat about, smoking, cracking jokes, the same as any military in the world. The old line 'hurry up and wait' came to mind. At night the officers would go to the first-class dining area and proceed to get drunk. I watched them doing karaoke with the Filipino cover band as the ship ploughed slowly and steadily to their next assignment. 'Papua good,' they would say to me drunkenly, giving me a thumbs-up.

But it was in the dramatically picturesque harbour of Jayapura, with the town at the foot of hills that rise from the sea, that their true feelings could be seen on their faces. The military were gearing up with their backpacks and weapons. The transmigrants were loaded with their bundles and luggage. Most of them had never been to Papua before and, as I watched them gather their belongings, there was a seriousness that hadn't been there in the past few days. To put it simply, they were anxious and a little afraid to be leaving the ship. There was apprehension in the air. They felt a bit threatened because of the stories they had heard. They were heading off into the great unknown. Some of the transmigrants were committing to live in rural or remote areas. The soldiers anticipated being deployed to the mountains, which they considered a war zone. The soldiers disembarked first, as if to reassure the civilian passengers it was all okay. The civilians followed, and I sat and watched as they struggled down the wharf with their heavy loads and children in tow. No one looked too happy. Settling in a new land was just a chore to get through.

*

In 2002 I woke up in a guest house in Sentani, about 20 kilometres from the capital Jayapura. I'd gone there because I had to get an early flight the next day. I went outside to the small verandah to order a coffee and some water and have a cigarette. The same Indonesian bloke was still there. He had obviously been there all night. He was drowsy and had moved to the chairs on my verandah. I sat down next to him and said in my bad Indonesian, 'Long night, eh?' He was charged with watching me and making sure I didn't speak to anyone. I'd obliged him by buying a few beers and retreating to my room. I sat inside and tapped out a story for *The Bulletin* on a tiny device called a pocketmail. It was the size of a glasses case with a keyboard. All you had to do was find a landline to a number in Australia and it would use a fax signal to send your message.

After a cold wash in what they called a *mandi*, a tub of cold water you would ladle over yourself with a bucket, I dressed and headed off to find some transport into town so I could get to a phone and send my story. And as I walked the 500 metres or so to the main road, I saw him and laughed to myself. I was walking so slowly that he was having trouble on his motorbike, trying to hold it in first gear without stalling as he followed me. I stopped to tie my shoelace just to mess with him.

I found a cab on the main road back to Jayapura. It was driven by a muscular black West Papuan with dreadlocks. He said, 'Are you John?' I said yes and we sat in silence as we passed the site of the previous week's demonstrations, the university where I had watched students fighting police, the spot where they had killed the leader Theys Eluay. All on the same road. He turned to me and said, 'We need some music, man.' I asked him what he had. He said, 'Marley, what about some Marley?' I said sure. In East Timor and Papua the young guys always played Marley on their outdated boomboxes or just on guitars as they sat around and drank the cheap but powerful palm wine when the power was off and the Indonesian curfews were on. They would go all night; there was nothing else to do.

He put the tape in (it was an old car) and looked in the rear-vision mirror. 'He is still following us,' he said of the Indonesian from the hostel on the motorbike. 'I am just going to go real slow.' He pressed the play button.

'*Won't you help to sing these songs of freedom? These songs of freedom. 'Cause all I ever had, redemption songs.*' I laughed until I almost cried. '*How long shall they kill our prophets?*' the song went on. We laughed all the way into the capital. He dropped me off at the main telephone exchange so I could send my report. He lost the guy in the traffic with some nifty lane-changing. He wouldn't take any money when I went to pay him. He just said, 'Do your job, man.' I never saw him again and never got his name.

After seeing the violence and knowing people the Indonesian security forces have killed, tortured and jailed in East Timor, Aceh and Papua, I cannot, as a human being and a journalist, walk away from this story and let the lies, obfuscations and outright atrocities against the people of those three Indonesian conflicts go unreported. I was in Iraq at the height of the American occupation, Sri Lanka at the height of the campaign to crush the Tamils, Burma at the height of the campaign against the Burmese people and the minorities who stood against the military, East Timor and Aceh under the Indonesians, Afghanistan in Taliban-controlled areas. But never have I seen a people more systematically oppressed and isolated than the West Papuans, by the Indonesian military and intelligence services.

I cannot walk away from the human rights workers, the local activists, the rebels who sacrificed their lives, the unarmed students and ordinary people who faced jail, beatings and bullets simply for marching in the street or attending a funeral or raising a flag. It is happening again now and it has to end. No amount of hiding the truth can stop the reality of the situation in Papua coming to light. They can build their road, but it will never be safe for the Indonesians or foreign workers to travel on as long as they continue to deny the people the right to what is theirs – their country and their resources. They can kill, jail and displace this generation, but there will be another one and another one. I hope I do not have to write this book again in twenty years, because if the Indonesians and the Australians and the UN continue their current policies in Papua, there will never be peace.

NOTES

1 Julian McKinlay King, 'A soul divided: the UN's misconduct over West Papua', *PORTAL Journal of Multidisciplinary International Studies,* Vol. 16, No. 1/2, 2019, pp. 59–81.

2 G.S. Rawlings in Julian McKinlay King, ibid., p. 69.

3 Frank Galbraith in Julian McKinlay King, ibid., p. 70.

4 Benny Giay, 'Finding a dignified resolution for West Papua', *The Conversation*, 6 May 2016.

5 Minorities at Risk Project, 'Chronology for Papuans in Indonesia', 2004, https://www.refworld.org/publisher,MARP,,IDN,469f389b1e,0.html.

6 Ken Roth, letter to Indonesian president Yudhoyono, 10 February 2006, https://www.hrw.org/news/2006/02/10/letter-indonesian-president-yudhoyono.

7 'Development aggression: observations on human rights conditions in the PT Freeport Indonesia Contract of Work areas with recommendations', Robert F. Kennedy Memorial Center for Human Rights, July 2002, http://wpik.org/Src/Development_Aggression.pdf.

8 Raymond Bonner, 'U.S. links Indonesian troops to deaths of 2 Americans', *The New York Times*, 30 January 2003.

9 Niniek Karmini, 'Villagers flee to escape shootings in Indonesia's Papua', *The Washington Post*, 7 March 2020.

10 Benny Wenda, 'Urgent alert: Indonesian military depopulating villages to protect Freeport gold mine', 10 March 2020, https://www.ulmwp.org/urgent-alert-indonesian-military-depopulating-villages-to-protect-freeport-gold-mine.

11 Mark Davis, email to author, 24 December 2018.

12 Mark Davis, 'Blood on the Cross', *Four Corners*, ABC-TV, 1999.

13 John Martinkus and Mark Davis, 'Chemical weapons dropped on Papua', *The Saturday Paper*, 22 December 2018–25 January 2019.

14 Pacific Media Watch, 'West Papua: sad plight of the Nduga internally displaced children', Asia Pacific Report, 21 January 2020; Kylie Grey, 'Villages torched, villagers tortured: extreme human rights violations in West Papua', *Dateline*, 12 September 2019.

15 Chantal Da Silva, 'West Papua flag day: why people around the world are raising the colours of a country that doesn't exist', *The Independent*, 1 December 2017.

16 Ben Doherty and Kate Lamb, 'West Papua independence petition is rebuffed at UN', *The Guardian*, 30 September 2017.

17 John Martinkus, 'Indonesia crackdown on West Papuan independence protest', *The Saturday Paper*, 14–20 May 2016.

18 'Lawmakers condemn foreign interference in Papua', *Jakarta Globe*, 6 May 2016.

19 Benjamin Strick and Famega Syavira, 'Papua unrest: social media bots "skewing the narrative"', BBC News, 11 October 2019.

20 Tom Allard and Jack Stubbs, 'Indonesian army wields internet "news" as a weapon in Papua', Reuters, 8 January 2020.

21 Stephen Wright, 'Papuans get independence petition to UN despite obstacles', AP, 31 January 2019.

22 Peter Boyle, 'UN receives petition calling for West Papua independence reform', *Green Left*, 28 January 2019.

23 Victor Mambor, 'Indonesia: Papua court convicts, sentences Polish man on treason charge', BenarNews, 2 May 2019.

24 'Indonesia jails Polish tourist in Papua for treason', BBC, 2 May 2019.

25 'Indonesia jails Polish tourist who met Papuan activists', *The Hindu*, 2 May 2019.

26 Liam Fox, 'Pacific Islands Forum leaders call for action on West Papua', *Pacific Beat*, ABC-TV, broadcast 19 August 2019.

27 Ben Doherty, 'Indonesia anger as West Papua independence raised at Pacific forum', *The Guardian*, 12 August 2019.

28 Liselotte Mas, 'Papuans turn monkey slur into a revolutionary symbol', France 24, 23 August 2019.

29 Maire Leadbeater, 'Deafening silence as West Papua crisis deepens', *The New Zealand Herald*, 20 November 2019.

30 Eka Kurniawan, 'Indonesia has a Papua problem', *The New York Times*, 26 September 2019.

31 Helen Davidson and Kate Lamb, 'West Papua: police investigate as bags of snakes thrown into student dormitory', *The Guardian*, 9 September 2019.

32 Antara, 'Soldier killed by gunmen on Papua New Guinea border', *The Jakarta Globe*, 30 December 2019.

33 Victor Mambor, 'Police officers accused of sexually harassing prisoner in Papua', *The Jakarta Post*, 5 December 2019.

34 Tom Allard, 'Indonesian human rights lawyer Koman refuses to be cowed on Papua', Reuters, 22 October 2019.

35 'Indonesian human rights lawyer wins prize for West Papua work', Radio New Zealand, 24 October 2019, https://www.rnz.co.nz/international/pacific-news/401682/indonesian-human-rights-lawyer-wins-prize-for-west-papua-work.

36 Victor Mambor, 'Indonesia: Papua flag raisers named as treason suspects', BenarNews, 4 December 2019.

CPSIA information can be obtained
at www.ICGtesting.com
Printed in the USA
LVHW111032210521
688113LV00004B/197